# Personal Best

Student's Book

A1 Beginner

Series Editor
**Jim Scrivener**

Author
**Graham Fruen**

# CONTENTS

| Unit | | | LANGUAGE | | | SKILLS | |
|---|---|---|---|---|---|---|---|
| | | | GRAMMAR | PRONUNCIATION | VOCABULARY | | |
| **1** | **My life** | | • the verb *be* (*I, you*)<br>• the verb *be* (*he, she, it*)<br>• the verb *be* (*we, you, they*) | • the alphabet<br>• word stress<br>• numbers | • greetings<br>• classroom language<br>• countries and nationalities<br>• numbers 0–100<br>• jobs<br>• adjectives (1) | **LISTENING**<br>• a video introducing the *Learning Curve* team<br>• listening for information about people<br>• contractions | **WRITING**<br>• completing a form<br>• capital letters<br>**PERSONAL BEST**<br>• a personal information form |
| | Hello | p4 | | | | | |
| 1A | Where's she from? | p6 | | | | | |
| 1B | Welcome to *Learning Curve*! | p8 | | | | | |
| 1C | We are the champions | p10 | | | | | |
| 1D | What's your email address? | p12 | | | | | |
| **2** | **People and things** | | • singular and plural nouns<br>• *this*, *that*, *these*, *those*<br>• possessive adjectives, *'s* for possession | • /ɪ/ and /iː/<br>• *'s* | • personal objects<br>• colours<br>• family and friends | **READING**<br>• an article about the Transport for London Lost Property Office<br>• preparing to read<br>• adjectives and nouns | **SPEAKING**<br>• asking for information politely<br>• telling the time<br>**PERSONAL BEST**<br>• asking for information at a cinema or airport |
| 2A | The man with only 15 things | p14 | | | | | |
| 2B | Lost! | p16 | | | | | |
| 2C | My family | p18 | | | | | |
| 2D | What time is it? | p20 | | | | | |

**1 and 2 — REVIEW and PRACTICE** p22

| Unit | | | GRAMMAR | PRONUNCIATION | VOCABULARY | | |
|---|---|---|---|---|---|---|---|
| **3** | **Food and drink** | | • present simple (*I, you, we, they*)<br>• present simple (*he, she, it*) | • *do you* /djuː/<br>• *-s* and *-es* endings | • food and drink<br>• days and times of day<br>• common verbs (1) | **LISTENING**<br>• A video about cafés around the world<br>• listening for times and days<br>• the sound /ə/ | **WRITING**<br>• punctuation<br>• linkers (*and*, *but*)<br>**PERSONAL BEST**<br>• a blog about a festival |
| 3A | Food for athletes | p24 | | | | | |
| 3B | Tea or coffee? | p26 | | | | | |
| 3C | Chocolate for breakfast! | p28 | | | | | |
| 3D | A special meal | p30 | | | | | |
| **4** | **Daily life** | | • adverbs of frequency<br>• present simple: *wh-* questions | • sentence stress<br>• question words | • daily routine verbs<br>• transport<br>• adjectives (2) | **READING**<br>• a text about New York's *citibikes*<br>• finding specific information<br>• *'s*: possession or contraction | **SPEAKING**<br>• being polite in shops<br>• shopping for food<br>**PERSONAL BEST**<br>• buying things in a restaurant, café or shop |
| 4A | Day and night | p32 | | | | | |
| 4B | My journey to work | p34 | | | | | |
| 4C | Where do you work? | p36 | | | | | |
| 4D | How can I help you? | p38 | | | | | |

**3 and 4 — REVIEW and PRACTICE** p40

| Unit | | | GRAMMAR | PRONUNCIATION | VOCABULARY | | |
|---|---|---|---|---|---|---|---|
| **5** | **All about me** | | • *can* and *can't*<br>• object pronouns | • *can* and *can't*<br>• /h/ | • common verbs (2)<br>• electronic devices<br>• activities | **LISTENING**<br>• a video about the importance of electronic devices<br>• listening for specific information<br>• sentence stress | **WRITING**<br>• describing yourself<br>• *because*<br>**PERSONAL BEST**<br>• an online profile |
| 5A | When can you start? | p42 | | | | | |
| 5B | I can't live without my phone | p44 | | | | | |
| 5C | I love it! | p46 | | | | | |
| 5D | My profile | p48 | | | | | |

Language App, unit-by-unit grammar and vocabulary games

# CONTENTS

| | | LANGUAGE | | | SKILLS | |
|---|---|---|---|---|---|---|
| | | GRAMMAR | PRONUNCIATION | VOCABULARY | | |
| **6** **Places** | | • there is/are<br>• prepositions of place | • linking consonants and vowels<br>• sentence stress | • places in a town<br>• parts of the body<br>• rooms and furniture | **READING**<br>• an article about art in public spaces<br>• reading in detail<br>• giving opinions | **SPEAKING**<br>• checking information<br>• asking for and giving directions<br>**PERSONAL BEST**<br>• a conversation asking for and giving directions |
| 6A City or village? | p50 | | | | | |
| 6B City art | p52 | | | | | |
| 6C An unusual home | p54 | | | | | |
| 6D Is there a post office near here? | p56 | | | | | |
| **5 and 6** — REVIEW and PRACTICE | p58 | | | | | |
| **7** **All in the past** | | • past simple: be<br>• past simple: regular verbs | • was/were<br>• -ed endings | • celebrities<br>• months and ordinals<br>• time expressions | **LISTENING**<br>• a video about Shakespeare and the theatre<br>• listening for dates<br>• linking consonants and vowels | **WRITING**<br>• writing informal emails<br>• sequencers<br>**PERSONAL BEST**<br>• an email about an interesting weekend |
| 7A When they were young | p60 | | | | | |
| 7B I was there in July | p62 | | | | | |
| 7C Famous decades | p64 | | | | | |
| 7D A weekend away | p66 | | | | | |
| **8** **Travel** | | • past simple: irregular verbs<br>• there was/were | • irregular past simple verbs<br>• sentence stress | • travel verbs<br>• weather and seasons<br>• nature | **READING**<br>• posts about an unusual trip on a travel website<br>• understanding the main idea<br>• modifiers | **SPEAKING**<br>• starting and ending a phone call at work<br>• buying a ticket<br>**PERSONAL BEST**<br>• a phone call buying a ticket |
| 8A Incredible journeys | p68 | | | | | |
| 8B Crazy weather! | p70 | | | | | |
| 8C Then and now | p72 | | | | | |
| 8D A trip to Canada | p74 | | | | | |
| **7 and 8** — REVIEW and PRACTICE | p76 | | | | | |
| **9** **Shopping** | | • present continuous<br>• how often + expressions of frequency | • -ing endings<br>• sentence stress | • clothes<br>• feelings<br>• shopping | **LISTENING**<br>• a video about how our clothes affect how we feel<br>• identifying key points<br>• filler words | **WRITING**<br>• describing a photo<br>• describing position<br>**PERSONAL BEST**<br>• an email describing a photo |
| 9A Street style | p78 | | | | | |
| 9B How do you feel? | p80 | | | | | |
| 9C Love it or hate it? | p82 | | | | | |
| 9D Garage sale | p84 | | | | | |
| **10** **Time out** | | • present continuous for future plans<br>• question review | • sentence stress<br>• intonation in questions | • free-time activities<br>• types of music and film<br>• sports and games | **READING**<br>• a listings page from an entertainment website<br>• scanning for information<br>• the imperative | **SPEAKING**<br>• showing interest<br>• asking about a tourist attraction<br>**PERSONAL BEST**<br>• a conversation about a tourist attraction |
| 10A What are you doing at the weekend? | p86 | | | | | |
| 10B What's on? | p88 | | | | | |
| 10C Royal hobbies | p90 | | | | | |
| 10D Where are we going now? | p92 | | | | | |
| **9 and 10** — REVIEW and PRACTICE | p94 | | | | | |

Grammar practice p96    Vocabulary practice p106    Communication practice p134    Irregular verbs p151

**Language App**, unit-by-unit grammar and vocabulary games

3

# UNIT 1 My life

**LANGUAGE** the verb *be* (*I, you*) ■ greetings ■ classroom language

## Hello

**1** ▶ 1.1 Read and listen. Match conversations 1–3 with pictures a–c.

1 **Wendy** Good morning. Are you Emma, the new teacher?
   **Emma** Yes, I am.
   **Wendy** I'm Wendy. Nice to meet you. You're in Class 3.
   **Emma** Thanks, Wendy. See you later.

2 **Emma** Hello, I'm Emma. What's your name?
   **Kiko** Hi, my name's Kiko.
   **Emma** Nice to meet you, Kiko.
   **Kiko** Are you a student here?
   **Emma** No, I'm not. I'm your teacher!

3 **Kiko** Emma, this is my friend, Misha.
   **Emma** Hello. Mmm, you aren't in Class 3, Misha.
   **Misha** No, I'm in Class 4 and I'm late! Goodbye!
   **Emma** Bye, Misha!

**2** Put the words from the conversations in the correct columns. Can you add any other words?

| Bye   Good morning | Hello | Goodbye |
|---|---|---|
| Hi   See you later | | |

**3 A** ▶ 1.2 Listen and repeat the highlighted phrases from the conversations in exercise 1. How do you say them in your language?

**B** Practise the conversations from exercise 1 in groups of four.

**4 A** Complete the sentences with the words in the box. Then check your answers in the conversations.

    're   'm   'm not   aren't   Are

1 I _____ Wendy.
2 You _____ in Class 3.
3 _____ you a student here?
4 No, I _____ .
5 You _____ in Class 3, Misha.

**B** ▶ 1.3 Listen and repeat the contractions in **bold**. Then read the Grammar box.

1 I am = **I'm**    2 You are = **You're**    3 You are not = **You aren't**

### Grammar   the verb *be* (*I, you*)

Positive:
**I'm** Wendy.
**You're** in Room 4.

Negative:
**You aren't** in Class 3.
**I'm not** a student.

Questions and short answers:
**Are you** a teacher?
Yes, **I am**.   No, **I'm not**.

**Go to Grammar practice:** the verb *be* (*I, you*), page 96

the verb *be* (*I*, *you*) ■ greetings ■ classroom language    LANGUAGE  **Hello**

**5  A** ▶ 1.5   Complete the conversation. Listen and check.

**Kiko**  Hello. What's ¹_____ name?
**Eleni**  ²_____ name's Eleni.
**Kiko**  Nice to ³_____ you, Eleni. I ⁴_____ Kiko.
**Eleni**  Nice to meet you, Kiko. ⁵_____ you a student here?
**Kiko**  ⁶ Yes, I _____ .

**B** In pairs, practise the conversation using your names.

**6** Introduce yourself and your partner to another pair.
  **A**  *Hello, I'm Caro. This is Pablo.*
  **B**  *Nice to meet you. My name's Malika and this is Petra.*

**7** ▶ 1.6   Read the phrases and write *Teacher* or *Student*. Listen and check.

1 _____  Open your books.
2 _____  Excuse me, what does 'late' mean?
3 _____  Sorry, I don't understand.
4 _____  Listen and repeat.
5 _____  How do you say 'buenos días' in English?
6 _____  Work in pairs.

Go to **Vocabulary practice:** classroom language, page 106

**8** ▶ 1.8   **Pronunciation:** the alphabet   Listen and repeat the sounds, words and letters.

| /eɪ/ | /iː/ | /e/ | /aɪ/ | /əʊ/ | /uː/ | /ɑː/ |
|---|---|---|---|---|---|---|
| late | meet | yes | my | no | you | class |
| Aa Hh Jj Kk | Bb Cc Dd Ee Gg Pp Tt Vv | Ff Ll Mm Nn Ss Xx Zz | Ii Yy | Oo | Qq Uu Ww | Rr |

**9** ▶ 1.9   Listen to the conversations. Write the names of the students.

Class 3
Student names:
1 _____
2 _____
3 _____

**ABC School of English**

Go to **Communication practice:** Student A page 134, Student B page 142

**10** Introduce yourself to five students. Ask the questions and write the answers.

What's your name?   How do you spell that?

**Personal Best**  Write a conversation between a teacher and a new student.

5

# 1 LANGUAGE  the verb *be* (*he, she, it*)  ■ countries and nationalities  ■ numbers 0–10

## 1A Where's she from?

**1 A** In pairs, match the flags with the countries.

A *What's a?*   B *I think it's Mexico.*

 a
 b
 c
 d
 e
 f
 g
 h

1 Argentina ____    3 China ____    5 Spain ____    7 the UK ____
2 Brazil ____        4 Mexico ____   6 Turkey ____   8 the USA ____

**B** ▶ 1.10  Listen, check and repeat.

**2 A** ▶ 1.11  Listen to the conversation. Repeat it in pairs.

A Where are you from?      A Where's Salta?
B I'm from Salta.          B It's in Argentina.

**B** In pairs, practise the conversation using the cities and countries.

Toledo / Spain   Izmir / Turkey   Harbin / China   York / the UK

*I'm from the UK. I'm British.*

**3** Look at the picture. Match the countries from exercise 1 with the nationalities.

1 British    _the UK_    4 American  _____    7 Turkish   _____
2 Spanish   _____    5 Argentinian _____   8 Brazilian _____
3 Mexican   _____    6 Chinese   _____

Go to Vocabulary practice: countries and nationalities, page 107

**4** ▶ 1.13  Do the quiz in pairs. Listen and check.

# THE C🌐UNTRIES QUIZ

**1** What nationality is Lewis Hamilton?
a He's British.
b He's American.

**5** Which sentence is correct?
a Sydney is the capital of Australia.
b Sydney isn't the capital of Australia.

**2** Where is Mount Fuji?
a It's in China.
b It's in Japan.

**6** Is *ceviche* Mexican or Peruvian?
a It's Mexican.
b It's Peruvian.

**3** Is this elephant from India or Africa?
a It's from India.
b It's from Africa.

**7** Where is the Bosphorus?
a It's in Turkey.
b It's in Russia.

**4** Is Elsa Pataky Russian?
a Yes, she is.
b No, she isn't.

**8** What nationality is Paulo Coelho?
a He's Italian.
b He's Brazilian.

the verb *be* (*he*, *she*, *it*) ■ countries and nationalities ■ numbers 0–10   LANGUAGE  1A

**5  A** Match the pronouns *he*, *she* and *it* with the people and things.

1  he           a  Elsa Pataky
2  she          b  *ceviche*
3  it           c  Lewis Hamilton

**B** Tick (✓) the form of the verb *be* that we use with *he*, *she* and *it*. Then read the Grammar box.

1  am ☐     2  is ☐     3  are ☐

### Grammar   the verb *be* (*he*, *she*, *it*)

**Positive:**
He's Japanese.
She's from Mexico.

**Negative:**
Barcelona **isn't** the capital of Spain.
She **isn't** Australian.

**Questions and short answers:**
**Is** it from India?
Yes, it **is**.   No, it **isn't**.

Go to Grammar practice: the verb *be* (*he*, *she*, *it*), page 96

**6  A**  ▶ 1.15  **Pronunciation: word stress**  Listen and repeat the words. Pay attention to the underlined stressed syllables.

Ja__pan__   Japa__nese__   __Mex__ico   __Mex__ican   __It__aly   I__tal__ian   __Tur__key   __Tur__kish

**B**  ▶ 1.16  Underline the stress in the countries and nationalities. Then listen, check and repeat.

1  I'm Brazilian.   2  She's from Germany.   3  It's Chinese.   4  Is he from Argentina?

**7**  In pairs, ask and answer the question *Where's … from?* about the people and things.

A  *Where's Zara from?*       B  *Is it Italian?*
A  *No, it isn't. It's Spanish.*

Zara

Ryan Gosling

Mercedes

Thalía

Neymar

Chow mein

**8  A**  ▶ 1.17  Listen and repeat the numbers.

zero/oh   one   two   three   four   five   six   seven   eight   nine   ten

**B**  ▶ 1.18  What are the international dialling codes for the countries? Listen and write the answers.

1  China       + _____
2  Colombia    + _____
3  India       + _____
4  Mexico      + _____
5  Spain       + _____
6  Turkey      + _____

Go to Communication practice: Student A page 134, Student B page 142

**9  A** In pairs, write six more quiz questions about countries and nationalities.

**B** Work with another pair. Ask and answer your quiz questions.

A  *What is the capital of Wales? a) It's Glasgow. b) It's Cardiff.*
B  *It isn't Glasgow – that's in Scotland. I think it's Cardiff.*
A  *That's right! Your turn.*

**Personal Best**  Write six sentences about people and things you like. Say where they are from.

7

**1 SKILLS** **LISTENING** listening for information about people ■ contractions ■ jobs

## 1B Welcome to *Learning Curve*!

**1** Match the jobs in the box with pictures a–f.

| doctor   engineer   office worker   police officer   taxi driver   waiter |

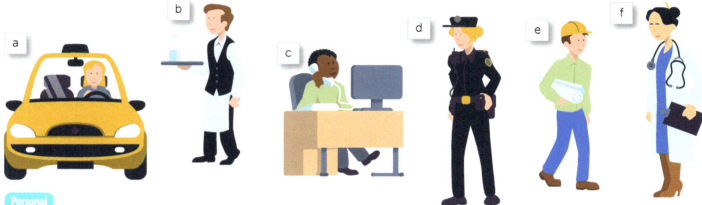

**Go to Vocabulary practice:** jobs, page 108

**2 A** ▶ 1.20   Look at the picture. Listen and complete the conversation.

**A** What's my job?
**B** Are you an [1]_____ ?
**A** No, I'm not. Try again!
**B** Are you a [2]_____ ?
**A** Yes, I am.

**B** In pairs, play 'What's my job?'.

**3** ▶ 1.21   Watch or listen to the start of a webshow called *Learning Curve*. Match the cities with the people.

1  New York         a  Simon, Kate, Marina
2  London           b  Ethan, Penny, Mohammed, Marc

 **Skill** listening for information about people

**We often listen to information about people.**
- Don't worry if you don't understand everything the speakers say.
- Read the questions and think about the information you need to listen for: name, job, nationality, etc.
- Listen for the verb *be*: *I'm ... / He's ... / She's ...* etc.

**4** ▶ 1.21   Read the Skill box. Watch or listen again and choose the correct information about the people.

**Simon Collins**
Nationality: British
Job: [1] *TV presenter / receptionist*

**Ethan Moore**
Nationality: [2] *American / British*
Job: TV presenter

**Penny Abernathy**
Nationality: English and [3] *Italian / Argentinian*
Job: TV presenter

**Marina Ivanova**
Nationality: Russian
Job: [4] *receptionist / teacher*

**Mohammed Bensallem**
Nationality: American
Job: [5] *TV presenter / office worker*

**Marc Kim**
Nationality: American
Job: [6] *doctor / IT specialist*

**Kate McRea**
Nationality: [7] *American / Argentinian*
Job: TV presenter

8

listening for information about people ■ contractions ■ jobs  **LISTENING**  **SKILLS**  **1B**

**5** ▶ 1.22 Watch or listen to the rest of the show. Who isn't in London now? Where is he/she?

**6** ▶ 1.22 Watch or listen again. Complete the information with countries and jobs.
1 Viktor: from: _____ job: _____ and _____
2 Sarah: from: _____ job: _____
3 Pedro: from: _____ job: _____

**7 A** In pairs, ask and answer the questions about the three people.

Where is … from?   What's his/her job?

**B** In pairs, ask and answer the questions about you.

Where are you from?   What's your job?

**8** ▶ 1.23 Listen and read what Kate says. How does she say the contractions in **bold**? What do they mean?

Hi, **I'm** Kate from *Learning Curve*. **What's** your name?

### Listening builder — contractions

In English, we often use contractions, especially when we speak.
**I'm** from the United States. = **I am** from the United States.
She **isn't** a student. = She **is not** a student.
**What's** your job? = **What is** your job?

**9** ▶ 1.24 Read the Listening builder. Listen and write the contractions.
1 _____ Spanish.    3 He _____ a doctor.   5 _____ an engineer.
2 _____ your name?  4 _____ from Japan.    6 The _____ here.

**10** ▶ 1.25 In pairs, look at the pictures of Jia and Luis. Guess the information about the people. Listen to the conversations and check.

job?   nationality?   Where now?

**11** Write the names of three friends or members of your family. In pairs, ask and answer questions about them.

A *Where's Saanvi from?*   B *She's from Nagpur.*
A *What's her job?*        B *She's an IT worker.*
A *Where is she now?*      B *She's in Mumbai.*

**Personal Best**  Choose five classmates and write their jobs, e.g. *Carla's a teacher.*

# 1 LANGUAGE — the verb *be* (we, you, they) ■ numbers 11–100 ■ adjectives (1)

## 1C We are the champions

**1 A** Write the numbers in the box in the correct order.

| sixteen   thirteen   fourteen   seventeen   twelve   twenty   ~~eleven~~   fifteen   nineteen   eighteen |

*eleven,* _____

**B** Look at the pictures and read the numbers. Tick (✓) the numbers that are correct.

1  twenty-three ☐   2  fifty-four ☐   3  eighty-six ☐   4  sixty-eight ☐   5  one hundred ☐   6  thirty ☐

**Go to Vocabulary practice:** numbers 0–100, page 111

**2 A** In pairs, ask and answer the question *How old is …?* for the people in the picture.

A  *How old is Kyle?*       B  *I think he's 40.*

**B** ▶ 1.27  Listen and write the ages.

Kyle _____    Martin _____    Lorna _____

**3 A** Look at the picture. What do you know about the rock band Queen? Do you know any songs or the names of the band members?

**B** Read the introduction to the interview. What is the name of the band?

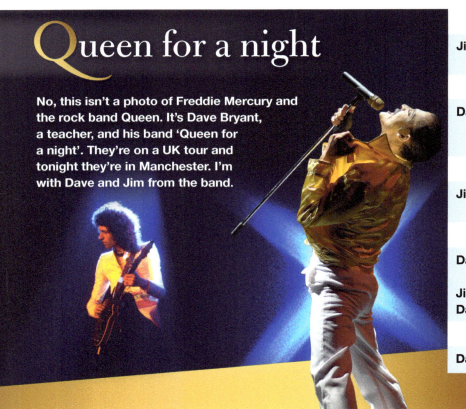

## Queen for a night

No, this isn't a photo of Freddie Mercury and the rock band Queen. It's Dave Bryant, a teacher, and his band 'Queen for a night'. They're on a UK tour and tonight they're in Manchester. I'm with Dave and Jim from the band.

**So Jim, are you all teachers?**

**Jim**  No, we aren't. I'm an engineer and Ed and Mick are doctors.

**And where are you from?**

**Dave**  I'm from London, Jim and Ed are from Oxford and Mick's from Bristol. We're old friends from university.

**How's the tour?**

**Jim**  It's good, but it's hard. It's a big tour – fourteen cities – and we aren't so young now!

**Really? How old are you?**

**Dave**  Mick and I are forty-seven. And you and Ed are fifty …
**Jim**  I'm not fifty! Ed's fifty … I'm forty-nine.
**Dave**  Oh yes. Sorry, Jim!

**And what's your favourite Queen song?**

**Dave**  That's easy! It's *We Are the Champions*!

the verb *be* (*we, you, they*) ■ numbers 11–100 ■ adjectives (1)    **LANGUAGE  1C**

**4** ▶ 1.28  Read and listen to the interview. Complete the information about the band.

|      | Dave | Jim | Ed | Mick |
|------|------|-----|----|------|
| job  |      |     |    |      |
| city |      |     |    |      |
| age  |      |     |    |      |

**5 A** Read the sentences from the interview. Match the people in **bold** with the pronouns *we*, *you* and *they*.

1 **Mick and I** are forty-seven. ____   2 **Jim and Ed** are from Oxford. ____   3 And **you and Ed** are fifty. ____

**B** Tick (✓) the form of the verb *be* we use when we talk about more than one person. Then read the Grammar box.

a  am / am not ☐     b  is / isn't ☐     c  are / aren't ☐

📖 **Grammar**   the verb *be* (*we, you, they*)

Positive:              Negative:                       Questions and short answers:
We**'re** old friends.     We **aren't** young.              **Are** you all teachers?
They**'re** on a UK tour.  They **aren't** the rock band Queen.   Yes, we **are**.   No, we **aren't**.

Go to Grammar practice: the verb *be* (*we, you, they*), page 96

**6 A** ▶ 1.30  **Pronunciation:** numbers  Listen and repeat the numbers. Pay attention to how the stress changes.

1  a  thir**teen**     b  **thir**ty       2  a  four**teen**     b  **for**ty       3  a  fif**teen**     b  **fif**ty

**B** ▶ 1.31  Listen and tick (✓) the numbers you hear. Listen again and repeat.

1  a  He isn't 16. ☐    b  He isn't 60. ☐    3  a  We aren't 17. ☐    b  We aren't 70. ☐
2  a  She's 18. ☐       b  She's 80. ☐       4  a  They're 19. ☐      b  They're 90. ☐

Go to Communication practice: Student A page 134, Student B page 142

**7** Match adjectives 1–4 from the text with their opposites in the box.

    bad   small   old   difficult

1  young _____     2  good _____     3  big _____     4  easy _____

Go to Vocabulary practice: adjectives (1), page 109

**8** Describe the pictures in pairs. Use positive and negative forms.

*Picture a: They're big. They aren't small.*

   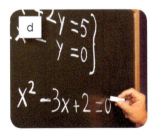

**9 A** In small groups, imagine you are in a band and complete the table.

| The name of the band | Your names | Your ages | Nationalities |
|----------------------|------------|-----------|---------------|
|                      |            |           |               |

**B** Work with another group. Interview each other about your bands.

( What's the name of your band? )  ( What are your names? )  ( How old are you? )  ( Where are you from? )

**Personal Best**  Write a short paragraph about a band you like.

# 1 SKILLS  WRITING  completing a form ■ capital letters

## 1D What's your email address?

**1** Match the places in the box with pictures a–c.

hotel   car rental office   gym

**2 A** Look at the form. Match it with one of the pictures in exercise 1.

**B**  1.33  Listen to the conversation. Which piece of information in the form is **incorrect**?

### Customer Information     CARS-4-U

| Title | MR ✓  MRS ☐  MS ☐ | | |
|---|---|---|---|
| Surname | Martin | First name(s) | Louis |
| Nationality | French | Date of birth | 17/06/1980 |
| Address | 35 Rue Pasteur, Paris | | |
| Postcode | 75099 | | |
| email address | louis.martin@mymail.com | | |
| Phone number | 33 1 80 26 58 | | |

### Skill | completing a form

**When you complete a form, read all the instructions and sections carefully.**
- Use the correct *title*. *Mr* = a man, *Mrs* = a married woman, *Ms* = a woman (married or unmarried).
- Your *surname* is your family name.
- Write your *date of birth* in numbers: the day/the month/the year: *13/09/1995*.
- For email addresses: @ = 'at' and .com = 'dot com'.

**3** Read the Skill box. Match sections 1–9 with information a–i.

1 postcode
2 date of birth
3 address
4 surname
5 first name
6 email address
7 title
8 phone number
9 nationality

a Smith
b M42 3GN
c Ms
d s.smith@cjbrooks.com
e 07700 900 357
f 23/11/1988
g British
h Sarah
i 36 Charles Street, Manchester

12

completing a form ■ capital letters  **WRITING**  SKILLS  **1D**

**4** In pairs, ask and answer questions about you, using the information in exercise 3.
  A *What's your surname?*  B *It's Taylor.*
  A *How do you spell that?*  B *It's T-A-Y-L-O-R.*

**5** Look at answers a–i in exercise 3. Tick (✓) the information with capital letters.
  1 first name ☐    3 email address ☐    5 street names ☐
  2 surname ☐      4 nationality ☐      6 cities ☐

### Text builder  capital letters

In English, we use capital letters (*A*, *B*, *C*, *D*, etc.) for the following:
- the first word in a sentence: *What's your name?*
- the personal pronoun *I*: *Hello, I'm Robert.*
- the names of people and places: *Emma is from Oxford.*
- countries, nationalities and languages: *We're from China. We're Chinese.*
- postcodes: *SN2 5EF*

**6** **A** Read the Text builder. Find one **incorrect** capital letter in each sentence.
  1 My friend Lena is American. She's From Florida.
  2 Hello, I'm Antonio. I'm a new Student.
  3 Our Address is 173 London Avenue, Manchester, M73 6XL.
  4 This is Mesut. He's from Turkey and he's Twenty-one.

**B** Rewrite the sentences with capital letters.
  1 what's his job? is he a doctor?  _____
  2 my address is 3 white street, glasgow gl33 4sc.  _____
  3 they aren't from germany. they're from poland.  _____
  4 i'm your new english teacher. my name's jack.  _____

**7** **A** PREPARE Look at the form. Check that you understand all the information you need to write.

**B** PRACTISE Complete your form. Remember to use capital letters correctly.

**C** PERSONAL BEST Swap your form with a partner. Is it clear and easy to read? Are the capital letters correct?

**Personal Best**  Design a form for a gym. Complete it with information about a family member.

13

# UNIT 2 People and things

**LANGUAGE** singular and plural nouns ■ *this*, *that*, *these*, *those* ■ personal objects

## 2A The man with only 15 things

**1** ▶ 2.1 In pairs, match the words in the box with objects a–f. Listen and check.

a book   a bag   keys   a watch   an umbrella   a camera

 a
 b
 c
 d
 e
 f

Go to Vocabulary practice: personal objects, page 110

**2** Look at exercise 1 and answer the questions. Then read the Grammar box.

1 Which noun do we use with *an*? _____
2 Which noun is plural? _____

### Grammar — singular and plural nouns

Singular nouns:   *a key*     *an umbrella*   *a watch*
Plural nouns:     *keys*      *umbrellas*     *watches*

Go to Grammar practice: singular and plural nouns, page 97

**3 A** Imagine you live with only 15 things. What are your 15 things?
**B** Read the text. Are your 15 things the same as Andrew's?

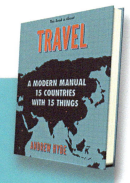

## 15 countries with 15 things

This is Andrew Hyde, and that's his book: *15 countries with 15 things*. Andrew is from Colorado in the USA and he's a writer and traveller. And it's true – he's a man with only 15 things!

**THESE ARE HIS 15 THINGS:**

| 1 ___ bag | 6 ___ wallet | 13 ___ shoes |
| 2 ___ smartphone | 7 ___ jacket | 14 ___ towel |
| 3 ___ camera | 8 ___ trousers | 15 ___ wash bag |
| 4 ___ iPad | 9 & 10 ___ shirts | |
| 5 ___ sunglasses | 11 & 12 ___ shorts | |

Andrew is back in the USA now, but is he happy with just those 15 things? Yes, he says. Life is easy without a lot of things.

singular and plural nouns ■ *this, that, these, those* ■ personal objects  **LANGUAGE 2A**

**4** Look at the list of Andrew's things again. Write *a* or *an* for singular nouns, and – for plural nouns.

**5** Complete the sentences from the text with the pronouns in the box. Which words do we use with singular nouns? Which ones with plural nouns? Then read the Grammar box.

that   those   this   these

1 _____ is Andrew Hyde.
2 _____'s his book.
3 _____ are his 15 things.
4 Is he happy with just _____ 15 things?

**Grammar**   *this, that, these, those*

**Things that are near us:**
*This* is my bag.
*These* are my keys.

**Things that aren't near us:**
*That*'s my car.
*Those* are my friends.

Go to Grammar practice: *this, that, these, those,* page 97

**6 A** ▶ 2.5   **Pronunciation:** /ɪ/ and /iː/   Listen and repeat the sounds and words.

/ɪ/   this   it   is   six
/iː/  these  he   three  keys

**B** ▶ 2.6   In pairs, say the sentences. Listen, check and repeat.

1 This is my city.
2 These are my keys.
3 Is that tree Japanese?
4 She's six and he's three.

Go to Communication practice: Students A and B page 135

**7** Choose the correct words to complete the text.

### What's in your bag?

**Maria Clara, office worker, Rio de Janeiro**
[1] *This / These* is my bag and [2] *this / these* are my things. This [3] *is / are* my book. It's in English! [4] *These / That* are my keys. [5] *This / These* key is for my house and [6] *that / those* key is for my car. [7] *This is / That's* my car over there – it's [8] *a / an* sports car! What's this? It's [9] *a / an* umbrella. It's very small! And the last thing? These are [10] *a / –* sunglasses!

**8 A** ▶ 2.7   Listen and match conversations 1–3 with pictures a–c.

**B** ▶ 2.7   Complete the phrases from the conversations with *this, that, these* and *those*. Listen again and check.

1 Jack    What's _____?
2 Woman  Jorge, who's _____ over there?
3 Man    Hi, Karen. What are _____?

Helen   _____ is my bag.
Jorge   _____'s Sergio.
Karen   _____ are my cameras.

**9** Put some things from your bag on the desk. In pairs, ask and answer questions about the things.

A *What's that?*
B *This is a book. It's in Spanish.*
A *And what are those?*
B *These are my keys.*

   Write about the things in your bag, as in exercise 7.

# 2 SKILLS READING preparing to read ■ adjectives and nouns ■ colours

## 2B Lost!

**1 A** Match the words in the box with the colours.

> blue   brown   green   orange   pink   red

**Go to Vocabulary practice:** colours, page 110

**B** In pairs, point to objects in the classroom. Ask and answer *What colour is that/are those...?*

A  *What colour are those books?*   B  *They're orange.*

### Skill — preparing to read

Before you read a text, look at other information to help you prepare.
- Think about the style of the text. Is it from a magazine, a website, a letter?
- Look at the pictures. What people, places and things can you see?
- Read the title. What does it mean?

**2 A** Read the Skill box. What do you think the text on page 17 is about? Tick (✓) a, b or c.

a  lost tourists in London ☐   b  transport in London ☐   c  lost objects in London ☐

**B** Read the text quickly and check your answer.

**3** Read the text again. Are the sentences true (T) or false (F)?

1  The Lost Property Office is in London.  ____
2  The objects are all from buses.  ____
3  Tim Carlisle is a tour guide every day.  ____
4  The laptop is new.  ____
5  All the instruments are expensive.  ____
6  The £15,000 is in the office now.  ____

**4** Complete the sentences with the words in the box. Check your answers in the text.

> expensive   violin   guitars   cheap

1  These _____ are _____ .   2  That's an _____ _____ .

### Text builder — adjectives and nouns

**adjective + noun:**  *£15,000 in a **brown** envelope*.
**noun + be + adjective:**  *This **laptop** is **new***.

**Look!** Adjectives don't change with plural nouns: *It's an **expensive** instrument*. *They're **expensive** instruments*.

**5** Read the Text builder. Order the words to make sentences.

1  good  it's  a  camera  _____
2  sunglasses  they're  expensive  _____
3  green  bag  the  is  _____
4  are  the  brown  wallets  _____
5  fast  a  it's  car  _____

**6 A** ▶ 2.9  Read and listen to the conversation in a Lost Property Office.

**B** In pairs, change the highlighted words and have a new conversation.

A  Hello, can I help you?
B  Do you have my wallet? It's a small, black wallet. It's expensive.
A  One moment. Is this your wallet?
B  Yes, that's it!

preparing to read ■ adjectives and nouns ■ colours    **READING**   SKILLS   **2B**

# Lost in London

22,000 mobile phones, 12,000 credit cards, a green 'Incredible Hulk' toy, £15,000 in a brown envelope …

These are some of the things in the Transport for London Lost Property Office. Every year, 300,000 objects are lost on buses, trains and taxis in the city. I'm at the office in central London, and with me is Tim Carlisle. Tim is a worker here, but today he's my tour guide.

'Look at all these things — wallets, glasses, bags, shoes, mobile phones — they're all here,' Tim tells me. 'Look at this laptop — it's new.'

In a different part of the office are musical instruments. 'These guitars are cheap, but that's an expensive violin,' he says.

'What's over there?' I ask.

'Those are umbrellas. Big umbrellas, small umbrellas, blue umbrellas, pink umbrellas …'

'And what about the envelope with £15,000?' I ask. 'Is it still here?'

'No,' Tim says. 'An old man collected it last month. He's 80 years old and he doesn't like banks!'

And that's the end of my tour. It's time for me to go. Now, where's my phone?

**Personal Best**   Write a conversation in a Lost Property Office.

# 2 LANGUAGE — possessive adjectives, 's for possession ■ family and friends

## 2C My family

**1** Match the people in the box with pictures a–d.

| husband and wife | mother and son | father and daughter | brother and sister |

**2** Put the words from exercise 1 in the correct columns.

| Male ♂ | Female ♀ |
| --- | --- |
| *brother* | *sister* |

Go to Vocabulary practice: family and friends, page 111

**3 A** Discuss the questions in pairs.
1 Are you from a big family or a small family?
2 Do you live with your family?
3 Does anyone in your family live in a different city or country?

**B** Read the text quickly. What is Laura's family situation? Is she sad about it?

## Long-distance families

Are you part of a 'long-distance' family? Are your brothers or sisters in a different city or country? Are you a long way from your parents or children? Tell us your stories.

### Laura Wickham

Hi! My name's Laura. My husband Seamus and I are long-distance parents! We live in Cork in Ireland. Our daughter Amy is 30 years old and she's in Australia. Our son Conor is 26 years old and he's in the USA.
Amy and Conor are a long distance from us, but their lives are very interesting. Amy's an IT worker in Perth. Her husband Pete is from there. He's an engineer. Pete is Australian. Conor's a surfing teacher in Los Angeles. He loves California and its beautiful beaches, so it's his dream job! Conor's girlfriend Nicole is a Hollywood actor … well, that's her dream. At the moment, she's a waitress.
We're on Skype a lot with our children, but it's difficult with the time differences. Am I sad that they're so far away? Sometimes, but the important thing is that they're happy.

**4** Read the text again. Match the information with the people.

1 This person is 30 years old.          a Seamus
2 This person is a waitress.            b Amy
3 This person lives in Cork.            c Pete
4 This person is a surfing teacher.     d Conor
5 This person is Australian.            e Nicole

possessive adjectives, 's for possession ■ family and friends    **LANGUAGE**  **2C**

**5** Complete the sentences from the text with the words in the box.

our  my  her  its  his  their

1 _____ name's Laura.
2 _____ son Conor is 26 years old.
3 _____ lives are very interesting.
4 _____ husband Pete is from there.
5 He loves California and _____ beautiful beaches.
6 It's _____ dream job!

**6 A** Choose the correct option to complete the sentence from the text.

*Conor's / Pete's / Seamus's* girlfriend Nicole is a Hollywood actor.

**B** What ending do we add to names and nouns to show possession? Read the Grammar box.

**Grammar**  possessive adjectives, 's for possession

**Possessive adjectives:**

| I | my: | I'm a teacher. **My** name's Karen. |
| you | your: | Are you OK? **Your** phone's broken. |
| he | his: | He's a tour guide. **His** job's interesting. |
| she | her: | She's Chinese, but **her** husband's British. |
| it | its: | Sydney's a great city. **Its** beaches are beautiful. |
| we | our: | We're in Class 3 and **our** teacher's very good! |
| they | their: | Jo and Ben aren't here. They're in **their** car. |

**'s for possession:**

**Kim's** mother is from Germany.
Is this **Amy's** book?
**My son's** new phone is expensive.

Go to Grammar practice: possessive adjectives, 's for possession, page 97

**7 A** ▶ 2.12 **Pronunciation:** 's Listen and repeat. Pay attention to the 's sound.

son's    daughter's    Amy's    Conor's    my husband's    my sister's

**B** ▶ 2.13 In pairs, say the sentences. Then listen, check and repeat.

1 My husband's name is Felipe.
2 Our son's girlfriend is French.
3 My wife's parents are from Canada.
4 Sara's brother's girlfriend is a doctor.

Go to Communication practice: Student A page 135, Student B page 143

**8** ▶ 2.14 Look at the people. In pairs, guess their relationship. Listen and check.

**A** *I think Jim is Tom Hanks's son.*    **B** *Yes, or maybe he's his brother.*

Tom Hanks

Victoria Beckham

Will Smith

Shakira

Andy Murray

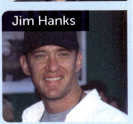
Jim Hanks

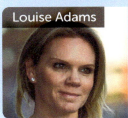
Louise Adams

Jaden Smith

Gerard Piqué

Judy Murray

**9** Choose five people in your family and write down their names. In pairs, ask and answer questions about the people.

**A** *Who is Azra?*    **B** *She's my brother's wife.*

Who is he/she?    How old is he/she?    What is his/her job?

**Personal Best**  Write a description of your family.

## 2 SKILLS  SPEAKING  asking for information politely ▪ telling the time

## 2D What time is it?

**1 A** ▶ 2.15  In pairs, match the times in the box with the clocks. Listen and check.

> five o'clock   ten past eight   quarter past ten   half past six   quarter to twelve   five to four

1 _____  2 _____  3 _____  4 _____  5 _____  6 _____

**B** ▶ 2.16  Complete the times. Listen, check and repeat.

1 It's eleven _____.  2 It's _____ three.  3 It's _____ twelve.  4 It's _____ nine.

**2 A** ▶ 2.17  Watch or listen to the start of *Learning Curve*. Choose the correct options to complete the sentences.

1 Kate is ____.
  a at home    b on holiday    c at work
2 ____ are on the phone.
  a Kate's parents    b Kate's friends    c Kate's brothers
3 They are in ____.
  a Boston    b Los Angeles    c London
4 Kate has ____ and a sister.
  a no brothers    b one brother    c two brothers

**B** ▶ 2.17  Watch or listen again and answer the questions.

1 What time is it in London? _____
2 What time is it in Los Angeles? _____

### Conversation builder  telling the time

**Asking for the time:**
What time is it?       What time's the film?
What's the time?       What time's the next bus?

**Talking about times:**
It's ten o'clock.         The film is at twenty past eight.
It's seven a.m./p.m.      The bus is in ten minutes.

**3 A** Read the Conversation builder. Match the questions with pictures a–d.

 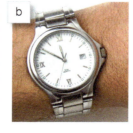    

1 What's the time? ____
2 What time is *The Simpsons*? ____
3 What time is it in New York? ____
4 What time's the train to Birmingham? ____

**B** Ask and answer the questions in pairs.

asking for information politely ■ telling the time  **SPEAKING**  **SKILLS**  **2D**

**4** ▶ 2.18  Watch or listen to the rest of the show. Match the times in the box with the people.

8.15   9.00   3.00   8.45   12.30

 Man 1
 Woman 1
 Woman 2
 Man 2
 Simon

**5 A** ▶ 2.18  Match the questions with the people from exercise 4. Watch or listen again and check.

1  When's the match?  _____
2  OK, what time is it?  _____
3  Excuse me. What time's the James Bond film? _____
4  Excuse me. What time is it, please? _____
5  Where's the 67 bus?  _____

**B**  Which questions are polite? Why?

> **Skill**  asking for information politely
>
> When you ask for information, it's important to be polite.
> • Use *Excuse me* or *Sorry* to get the person's attention.
> • At the end of the conversation, say *Thank you* or *Thanks*.
> • If you want to be extra polite, say *Please* at the end of questions.

**6** ▶ 2.19  Read the Skill box. In pairs, guess the missing words from the conversations. Listen and check.

**Woman 1**  ¹_____ . What time is it, ²_____ ?
**Kate**  It's 8.15. Quarter past.
**Woman 1**  Oh! I'm late. ³_____ very much.

**Woman 2**  ⁴_____ , what time is the 67 bus?
**Kate**  Next bus ... 8.45. It's in ten minutes.
**Woman 2**  Oh, 8.45, not 8.35. Ten minutes. OK. ⁵_____ .

**7**  In pairs, practise asking for information politely.

| Questions | Answers |
|---|---|
| what / the teacher's name | It's Leanne. |
| what time / next bus to Cambridge | It's at 12.20 p.m. |
| where / the museum | It's that building. |
| what / name of this restaurant | It's The Golden Dragon. |
| what / the school's phone number | It's 354 269. |

Go to Communication practice: Student A page 135, Student B page 143

**8 A** **PREPARE**  In pairs, choose the cinema or the airport and invent the missing information.

★ SILVER CINEMA ★

| FILM | TIME | SCREEN |
|---|---|---|
| Star Wars | ____ | ____ |
| Titanic | ____ | ____ |
| The Wizard of Oz | ____ | ____ |

Airport departures ✈  10:05

| Flight | Time | Gate |
|---|---|---|
| Stockholm | ____ | ____ |
| Beijing | ____ | ____ |
| Lima | ____ | ____ |

**B** **PRACTISE**  In pairs, ask and answer questions about the films or the flights. Remember to be polite.

**C** **PERSONAL BEST**  Invent information for the other situation and repeat the activity. Is your speaking better this time?

**Personal Best**  Write a conversation with a tourist in your local train or bus station.

21

# 1 and 2 REVIEW AND PRACTICE

## Grammar

1 Choose the correct options to complete the sentences.

1 Hi Laura, I _____ Khalid's brother. Nice to meet you.
  a 's
  b 're
  c 'm

2 How old _____ your grandfather?
  a are
  b is
  c am

3 _____ these your glasses?
  a Am
  b Is
  c Are

4 A Is your sister's boyfriend from Brazil?
  B No, _____ .
  a he isn't
  b she isn't
  c I'm not

5 A What's this?
  B It's _____ old book.
  a –
  b a
  c an

6 _____ my mother over there with the blue umbrella.
  a These are
  b This is
  c That's

7 My wife's a chef and this is _____ new restaurant.
  a she's
  b her
  c his

8 My _____ surname is Chen.
  a grandfather's
  b grandfather
  c grandfathers

2 Rewrite the sentences with the new words.

1 He's an English teacher.
  They *'re English teachers* .

2 These are my red pens.
  This _____ .

3 We're happy with our new tablets.
  I _____ .

4 Those expensive cars are Italian.
  That _____ .

5 I'm a student in India.
  She _____ .

6 My brother's an office worker and this is his bag.
  My brothers _____ and these _____ .

3 Choose the correct options to complete the text.

### A HOLLYWOOD FAMILY

[1] *These / This* is Zooey Deschanel. She's [2] *a / an* actor and a singer. [3] *She / Her* sister Emily is an actor too. She's in the TV show *Bones*. What [4] *'s / 're* their mother's job? An actor. And [5] *their / our* father's job? [6] *Her / His* job is in films too! That's not all – Zooey's [7] *sister's / sisters* husband is … an actor. They [8] *'re / 's* from California in the USA and they're a Hollywood family. They [9] *are / aren't* the only family like this. From Marlon Brando's family to Will Smith's family, they [10] *'m / 're* easy to find in Hollywood.

## Vocabulary

1 Put the words in the box in the correct columns.

| difficult engineer grandfather interesting IT worker mobile phone mother pencil receptionist small watch wife |

| Jobs | Adjectives | Family | Personal objects |
|---|---|---|---|
|  | *difficult* |  |  |

22

**REVIEW and PRACTICE 1 and 2**

**2** Circle the word that is different. Explain your answers.
1  black     new         orange       gold
2  chef      tour guide  TV presenter grandmother
3  French    Polish      Russian      Canada
4  fifty     thirteen    fourteen     seventeen
5  son       glasses     purse        keys
6  Hi        Bye         Hello        Good morning
7  bad       boring      ugly         happy
8  father    daughter    boyfriend    husband

**3** Choose the correct options to complete the sentences.
1  Jing Wei is _____ . She's from Shanghai.
   a doctor    b Chinese    c brother
2  Excuse me, what does 'building' _____ ?
   a say       b understand c mean
3  My sister's daughter is six and her _____ is four.
   a son       b children   c husband
4  That camera is very _____ .
   a new       b young      c sad
5  Russia is a very _____ country.
   a small     b easy       c big
6  I'm from _____ . I'm American.
   a the UK    b the USA    c Argentina
7  A It's ten past nine.
   B Sorry I'm _____ .
   a student   b teacher    c late
8  Macu is a _____ . She's in her car all day.
   a shop assistant  b taxi driver  c girlfriend
9  A What colour is a chef's hat?
   B It's _____ .
   a white     b small      c pink
10 The pages of this old _____ are yellow.
   a tablet    b wallet     c book

**4** Complete the conversation with the words in the box.

| nineteen | Germany | Italian | waitress |
| bag | student | girlfriend | later |

Max  Who's that girl with Frank? Is she his sister?
Sue  No. That's his new ¹_____ .
Max  Wow! Is she from here?
Sue  No, she's from ²_____ .
Max  She's beautiful. How old is she?
Sue  She's ³_____ .
Max  Is she a ⁴_____ at the university?
Sue  No, she's a ⁵_____ at the ⁶_____ restaurant in Green Road.
Max  Oh no, I'm late for class. See you ⁷_____ .
Sue  Hey … is that your ⁸_____ ?
Max  Yes, it is. Thanks!
Sue  Bye.

23

# UNIT 3 Food and drink

**LANGUAGE** present simple (*I, you, we, they*) ■ food and drink

## 3A Food for athletes

**1** ▶ 3.1 Put the words in the box in the correct columns. Listen and check.

| eggs | orange juice | meat | tea | coffee | bread | rice | water |

| We eat … | We drink … |
| --- | --- |

Go to Vocabulary practice: food and drink, page 112

**2** In pairs, talk about food and drink that you like and don't like.

 *I like meat.*     *I don't like coffee.*

**3 A** Look at the pictures. What food can you see? Is it healthy?

**B** Match pictures a and b with the athletes. Read the text quickly and check.

# Olympic Diets
What do Olympic athletes eat for breakfast, lunch and dinner? We talk to two very different athletes.

### Artem Petrenko, Weightlifter, Ukraine

**What do you eat for breakfast?**
For breakfast, I eat six eggs and three or four cheese sandwiches. I drink a litre of orange juice and three cups of coffee.

**What about lunch and dinner?**
I have lunch at 1.00 p.m. I eat a big bowl of pasta or rice and salad. For dinner, I eat meat – with potatoes and vegetables. During the day, I eat more sandwiches and fruit.

**That's a lot of food! What's your favourite food?**
Cheese. I love all cheese, and my favourite is Dutch cheese, like Gouda.

### Michelle Nelson, Marathon runner, Australia

**What do you eat for breakfast?**
For breakfast, I eat brown bread and fruit and I drink 'green juice' – it's juice with green vegetables and fruit. I'm a vegan, so I don't eat meat, eggs or fish and I don't drink milk.

**What about lunch and dinner?**
For lunch, I have a vegan burger with rice and salad. In the evening, I have dinner with my family. It's difficult because we don't like the same things! But we all eat pizza. My two sisters like cheese, but I have a vegan pizza – without cheese!

**Do marathon runners eat dessert?**
Yes, they do! Well, maybe not all of them … but I love dessert. It's my favourite part of the meal. I love carrot cake and vegan ice cream.

present simple (*I, you, we, they*) ■ food and drink    LANGUAGE  3A

**4** Read the text again and complete the sentences with the correct words.
1 What _____ you _____ for breakfast?
2 I _____ a litre of orange juice.
3 I _____ lunch at 1.00 p.m.
4 I _____ milk.
5 We _____ the same things.
6 _____ marathon runners _____ dessert?

**5 A** Look at the sentences in exercise 4 and answer the questions.
1 Which sentences are positive? ____ and ____
2 Which are negative? ____ and ____
3 Which are questions? ____ and ____

**B** Complete the rules. Then read the Grammar box.
1 We use _____ + verb in negative present simple sentences with *I, you, we* and *they*.
2 We use _____ + subject + verb in present simple questions with *I, you, we* and *they*.

### Grammar  present simple (*I, you, we, they*)

Positive:
I **drink** a lot of water.
We **eat** ice cream for dessert.

Negative:
You **don't drink** coffee.
They **don't like** vegetables.

Questions and short answers:
**Do** you **like** fish?
Yes, I **do**.   No, I **don't**.

Go to Grammar practice: present simple (*I, you, we, they*), page 98

**6** ▶ 3.4 **Pronunciation:** *do you* /djuː/ Listen and repeat the questions. Pay attention to the pronunciation of *do you* /djuː/.
1 Do you like pizza?   2 What do you eat for breakfast?   3 What food do you like?

**7 A** ▶ 3.5 Say the questions. Listen, check and repeat.
1 Do you like Mexican food?
2 Do you eat meat?
3 Do you drink tea?
4 Do you like chocolate?
5 What time do you have breakfast?
6 What do you have for lunch?

**B** Ask and answer the questions in pairs.

**8 A** ▶ 3.6 Complete the text with the verbs in brackets. Listen and check.

## Happy food

What food ¹_____ (you / like) after a difficult day? What
²_____ (you / eat) when you're sad? What's your 'happy food'?

I'm a student. After a difficult day at university, ³_____ (we / always have) ice cream. ⁴_____ (I / like) caramel – it's my favourite!
**Harriet, the UK**

My children are strange. ⁵_____ (they / not like) normal sandwiches. ⁶_____ (they / eat) banana and cheese sandwiches!
**Mike, Canada**

I'm a doctor. When I'm tired or sad, ⁷_____ (I / not eat) chocolate or pizza – it's bad for you. ⁸_____ (I / drink) green tea.
**Rosa, Argentina**

**B** In pairs, talk about your 'happy food'. What do you eat or drink when you're sad or tired?

Go to Communication practice: Student A page 136, Student B page 144

**9 A** Ask and answer questions in pairs.
1 like / Japanese food
2 drink / a lot of soft drinks
3 have / dinner with your family
4 eat / a lot of fruit
5 drink / coffee at night
6 eat / a lot of red meat

A *Do you like Japanese food?*   B *No, I don't. But I like Indian food.*

**B** Tell the class what you and your partner have in common.

*We don't like Japanese food, but we like Indian food.*

**Personal Best**  Write what you have for breakfast, lunch and dinner on a typical day.

# 3 SKILLS  LISTENING  listening for times and days ■ the sound /ə/ ■ days and times of day

## 3B Tea or coffee?

1 Complete the café sign with the days of the week.

Friday   Tuesday   Wednesday   Sunday

**Riverside Café**

We are open:
Monday    Closed
1 _____    9.00 a.m.–5.00 p.m.
2 _____    9.00 a.m.–5.00 p.m.
Thursday   Closed
3 _____    9.00 a.m.–9.00 p.m.
Saturday   10.00 a.m.–11.00 p.m.
4 _____    10.00 a.m.–4.00 p.m.

Hot food & sandwiches!
Coffee & cake!

**Go to Vocabulary practice:** days and times of day, page 116

2 Look at the sign in exercise 1 again. Are the sentences true (T) or false (F)?
   1 The café is open every day. ____
   2 It's open in the morning on Tuesday. ____
   3 It's open on Thursday afternoon. ____
   4 It's open in the evening on Friday. ____
   5 It's closed on Saturday night. ____
   6 It's closed in the evening on Sunday. ____

3 Ask and answer the questions in pairs.
   1 What day is it today?
   2 What day is it tomorrow?
   3 What day was it yesterday?
   4 What's your favourite day of the week?
   5 What's the worst day of the week?
   6 What's your favourite time of day?

4 A ▶ 3.8   Watch or listen to the first part of the show. Tick (✓) the sentence which is correct.
   1 People drink coffee in cafés and tea at home. ☐
   2 People drink tea and coffee all over the world. ☐
   3 People drink coffee in the morning and tea in the evening. ☐

B ▶ 3.8   Watch or listen again. Match the halves to make sentences.
   1 54% of Americans
   2 65% of those people
   3 35% of those people
   4 In the UK, people drink 165 million
   5 In the UK, people drink 70 million

   a cups of tea every day.
   b drink coffee at lunch or later.
   c drink coffee every day.
   d drink coffee in the morning.
   e cups of coffee every day.

listening for times and days ■ the sound /ə/ ■ days and times of day   LISTENING   SKILLS   3B

**5** ▶ 3.9   Watch or listen to the second part of the show. Match the people with the food and drink.

1  fish, rice, vegetables, tea, water  _____
2  biscuits, ice cream, coffee  _____
3  fish and chips and tea  _____
4  sandwich, crisps, biscuit, tea  _____
5  coffee, cereal  _____

**Skill**  listening for times and days

Listen carefully when people talk about times and days.
- Times and days can come at the beginning or end of a sentence: *On Friday, I go to the café. / I go to the café on Friday.*
- Some times and days sound similar: *It's three fifteen. / It's three fifty.*   *Today is Tuesday. / Today is Thursday.*

**6** ▶ 3.9   Read the Skill box. Watch or listen again and choose the correct options to complete the sentences.

1  **Kate:** It's *2.30 p.m. / 2.40 p.m.* here and I'm with Jolene.
2  **Jolene:** We come here every *Tuesday / Thursday*. It's my husband's favourite café.
3  **Jolene:** I drink coffee every *morning / evening*, but between 2.30 and *3.00 / 3.30*, I drink tea.
4  **Ioan:** The party's at *8.00 p.m. / 9.00 p.m.*
5  **Chan:** We're open *Monday / Sunday* through Friday from 11.00 a.m. until 10.00 p.m. And Saturday and Sunday from 10.00 a.m. until *7.00 p.m. / 11.00 p.m.*
6  **Kate:** It's *3.15 / 3.30* here and I have fish and chips from my favourite takeaway place!

**7**  In pairs, talk about what food and drink you have every day.
*I have a coffee at 10.00 in the morning.*

**8** ▶ 3.10   Listen to the extract from the show. How does Ethan pronounce *and*?

> I have a coffee **and** cereal.

**Listening builder**  the sound /ə/

The /ə/ sound is also called 'schwa'. It is very common in English in short unstressed words, like articles, prepositions and auxiliary verbs.

/ə/  /ə/           /ə/                    /ə/                         /ə/
<u>a</u> cup <u>of</u> tea   We have coffee <u>at</u> 9.00 p.m.   What time's <u>the</u> party?   <u>Does</u> she like fish?

**9** ▶ 3.11   Read the Listening builder. Then listen and complete the sentences.

1  I have _____ coffee every morning.
2  What _____ they eat?
3  They only drink tea _____ breakfast.
4  This one's _____ you.
5  I have two bottles _____ water.
6  I like fish _____ chips.

**10**  Think of a café that you like. In pairs, ask and answer the questions about the café.

What's its name?   Where is it?   When do you go there?
What do you eat or drink there?   What do other people have?   Why do you like it?

**Personal Best**   Write a description of your favourite restaurant or café.

27

# 3 LANGUAGE    present simple (he, she, it) ■ common verbs (1)

## 3C Chocolate for breakfast!

**1** Complete phrases 1–6 with the verbs in the box.

use   watch   have   do   make   say

1 ____ 'hello'   2 ____ a cat   3 ____ dinner   4 ____ exercise   5 ____ a computer   6 ____ TV

**Go to Vocabulary practice:** common verbs (1), page 113

**2** Ask and answer the questions in pairs.
1 you / live near the city centre?
2 you / work in an office?
3 you / make dinner at home every evening?
4 you / know three languages?
5 you / say 'hello' to a lot of people every day?
6 you / have brothers or sisters?

**3** ▶ 3.13   Look at the picture of Adam Young. What is his job? Read and listen to the text and check.

## THE BEST JOB IN THE WORLD?

From Monday to Friday, Adam Young eats chocolate at work. That's because Adam is a *chocolatier* (he makes chocolate). 'I love it,' he says. 'I think it's a great job!'
Adam lives in Perth in Scotland. He has a small shop and he makes all of his chocolates by hand. Does he have the best job in the world? This is his typical day.
'In the morning, I go to the shop early and make chocolate … I eat it for breakfast! Then we work here all day.'

Adam has an assistant, Shona. When he's in the kitchen with the chocolate, Shona works with the customers.
Adam does a lot of exercise – very important when you eat chocolate all day! In the evening, he changes his clothes and goes to the gym. Then he goes home, makes dinner and watches TV.
At the weekend, he studies Business – he says it's important for his job … but he doesn't eat chocolate!

**4 A** Choose the correct words to complete the sentences. What letter do we add to the verbs with *he*, *she* and *it* in positive sentences?
1 Adam Young *eat* / *eats* chocolate at work.
2 He *make* / *makes* all of his chocolates by hand.
3 I go to the shop early and *make* / *makes* chocolate.
4 I *eat* / *eats* it for breakfast!
5 Then we *work* / *works* here all day.
6 Shona *work* / *works* with the customers.

**B** Find the *he*/*she*/*it* forms of the verbs in the text.
1 say _____   3 have _____   5 change _____   7 watch _____
2 live _____   4 do _____    6 go _____       8 study _____

28

present simple (*he*, *she*, *it*)  ■  common verbs (1)  **LANGUAGE 3C**

**5** Find a question and a negative sentence in the text. Complete the rules then read the Grammar box.
1 We use _____ + verb in negative present simple sentences with *he/she/it*.
2 We use _____ + subject + verb in present simple questions with *he/she/it*.

📖 **Grammar** present simple (*he*, *she*, *it*)

**Positive:**
She **eats** fruit for breakfast.
He **watches** TV in the evening.
Maya **studies** English.

**Negative:**
He **doesn't work** in a school.
She **doesn't do** exercise.
My wife **doesn't like** chocolate.

**Questions and short answers:**
**Does** your house **have** a garden?
Yes, it **does**.   No, it **doesn't**.

**Look!** Some verbs are irregular: *do* > **does**, *go* > **goes**, *have* > **has**.

Go to Grammar practice: present simple (*he*, *she*, *it*), page 98

**6 A** ▶ 3.15 **Pronunciation:** *-s* and *-es* endings  Listen and repeat the sounds and words. Pay attention to the pronunciation of the *-s* and *-es* endings.
1 /s/    eats       works     makes
2 /z/    lives      goes      knows
3 /ɪz/   watches    uses      changes

**B** ▶ 3.16 Match the halves to make sentences. Listen, check and repeat.
1 She lives          a films in the afternoon.
2 He works           b in an office.
3 She watches        c a computer at work.
4 He says            d 'Hi' every day.
5 She makes          e in Tokyo.
6 He uses            f cakes at the weekend.

**7** ▶ 3.17 Complete the text with the correct form of the verbs in the box. Listen and check.

have   do   eat   say   work   make   go

## A VERY COOL JOB

Kirsten Lind ¹_____ at an ice cream company in Toronto. She ²_____ a great job – she's a food scientist and she ³_____ new flavours of ice cream. What's this week's new flavour? 'Potato crisps and chocolate! I don't like crisps, but lots of people love it,' Kirsten ⁴_____ . Kirsten ⁵_____ two or three litres of ice cream a week, so she ⁶_____ to the gym after work and she ⁷_____ a lot of sport at the weekend.

**8 A** Make questions about the text in exercise 7.
1 Kirsten / work / in a shop?           _____
2 she / have / an interesting job?      _____
3 she / eat / a lot of crisps?          _____
4 she / do / a lot of exercise?         _____

**B** Ask and answer the questions in pairs. Use short answers.

Go to Communication practice: Student A page 136, Student B page 144

**9** Choose three friends or family members and write down their names. Ask and answer the questions in pairs.
**A** *Who is Ivan?*            **B** *He's my uncle.*
**A** *Where does he live?*     **B** *He lives in …*

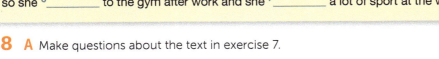

| Who is … ? | Where does he/she live? | Where does he/she work? |
| Does he/she like his/her job? | What does he/she do at the weekend? |

**Personal Best**  Think of someone with an interesting job and write a paragraph about him/her.

29

## 3 SKILLS   WRITING   punctuation ■ linkers (*and*, *but*)

### 3D A special meal

**1 A** Match the food in the box with the festivals in the pictures. What do you know about these festivals?

pancakes   chow mein   turkey   sweets

Thanksgiving, USA

Carnevale, Italy

Chinese New Year, China

Maslenitsa, Russia

**B** Think of some important festivals and celebrations in your country. What do people eat and drink?

**2** Look at the pictures in Arusha's blog. Which country is she from? How do people celebrate this festival? Read the text quickly and check.

# Arusha's Blog
MY POSTS | CONTACT ME | SEARCH

**About me**
Hi! I'm Arusha, I'm 25 and I live in Kerala in India. Welcome to my blog!

**Festival time**
We have lots of festivals in India and my favourite is Onam.
In the afternoon, we have a big meal with lots of food – some people have 24 dishes or more. We eat curry, rice, vegetables and fruit, but we don't eat meat. We eat the food on a big banana leaf.

It's traditional to have lunch at home, but these days some people go to restaurants. In my family, we eat at my brother's house. After the meal, we meet friends, we listen to music and we watch the tiger dance. What's my favourite thing about Onam? It's a really happy time and the food is great.

**3** Read the text again and answer the questions.

1  What is the name of the festival?
2  When do people have the meal?
3  What food does Arusha eat?
4  What doesn't she eat?
5  Where does she have lunch?
6  What does she do after the meal?

punctuation ■ linkers (*and*, *but*) **WRITING** **SKILLS** **3D**

**4** Read the Skill box. Find an example of each type of punctuation in the text on page 30.

> **Skill** | **punctuation**
>
> It's important to use the correct punctuation to help people understand your writing.
>
> . **full stop:** We use this at the end of a sentence.
> , **comma:** We use this to separate ideas and after times.
> ? **question mark:** We use this at the end of a question.
> ' **apostrophe:** We use this in contractions and in *'s* for possession.
> A **capital letters:** (see the Text builder on page 13)

**5** Rewrite the text about Chinese New Year with the correct punctuation and capital letters.

**whats your favourite festival**

my names wu and im from nanjing in china my favourite festival is chinese new year its a national holiday and people dont work we have a big party with all the family and in the evening we eat meat fish rice and vegetables my mother makes a special cake and we give money to the children in the family

**6** Choose the correct words to complete the sentences from Arusha's blog. Check your answers in the text.
1 We eat curry, rice, vegetables and fruit, *and* / *but* we don't eat meat.
2 It's a really happy time *and* / *but* the food is great.

> **Text builder** | **linkers (*and*, *but*)**
>
> We use *and* and *but* to link sentences.
> **To add information:** *We dance **and** we listen to music.*
> **To contrast different ideas:** *Some people go to restaurants, **but** our family eats at home.*

**7** Read the Text builder. Complete the sentences with *and* or *but*.
1 We go to my grandmother's house every Sunday _____ we have a big meal.
2 This restaurant is very expensive, _____ the food isn't good.
3 I drink tea and fruit juice, _____ I don't drink coffee.
4 Claire works in the morning, _____ she doesn't work in the afternoon.
5 My uncle lives in Los Angeles, _____ he isn't American.
6 He does sport _____ he goes to the gym.

**8 A** **PREPARE** Choose a festival in your country where food is important. Think about these questions.
• When is the festival?
• What do people eat and drink?
• Where do you eat and who with?
• What do you do before and after the meal?

**B** **PRACTISE** Write a blog about the festival. Link your sentences with *and* and *but*.

**C** **PERSONAL BEST** Swap your blog with your partner. Check the grammar and punctuation. Are the present simple verbs correct? Does your partner use *and* and *but* correctly?

**Personal Best** Think of a special meal. Write three sentences about it with *and* and three sentences with *but*.

31

# UNIT 4

# Daily life

**LANGUAGE** adverbs of frequency ■ daily routine verbs

## 4A Day and night

**1 A** ▶ 4.1 Match the phrases in the box with pictures a–e. Listen and check.

start work   finish work   go to bed   get home   get up

**B** In pairs, say what time you do the activities.

A *I get up at 6.30.*   B *That's early! I get up at 8.30.*

**Go to Vocabulary practice:** daily routine verbs, page 114

**2** Look at the pictures and guess the answers to the questions. Read the text and check.

1 What is the relationship between the two people?
2 What are their jobs?
3 Are their routines similar or different?

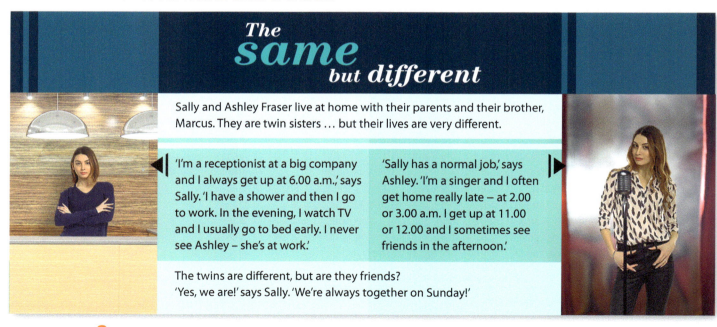

### The same but different

Sally and Ashley Fraser live at home with their parents and their brother, Marcus. They are twin sisters … but their lives are very different.

'I'm a receptionist at a big company and I always get up at 6.00 a.m.,' says Sally. 'I have a shower and then I go to work. In the evening, I watch TV and I usually go to bed early. I never see Ashley – she's at work.'

'Sally has a normal job,' says Ashley. 'I'm a singer and I often get home really late – at 2.00 or 3.00 a.m. I get up at 11.00 or 12.00 and I sometimes see friends in the afternoon.'

The twins are different, but are they friends?
'Yes, we are!' says Sally. 'We're always together on Sunday!'

**3** Complete the sentences with the adverbs of frequency in the box. Check your answers in the text.

always   sometimes   usually   never   often

1 I _____ see Ashley.
2 I _____ see friends in the afternoon.
3 I _____ get home really late.
4 I _____ go to bed early.
5 I _____ get up at 6.00 a.m.

32

adverbs of frequency ■ daily routine verbs    LANGUAGE    **4A**

**4 A** Put the adverbs of frequency in the box in the correct order.

> sometimes   usually   never

100% ──────────────────────────────────── 0%

always    1 _____    often    2 _____    3 _____

**B** Read the sentences in exercise 3 again. Do the adverbs of frequency come before or after the verbs? Read the Grammar box.

📖 **Grammar**  adverbs of frequency

100%
always:    I **always** have breakfast at home.
usually:   She **usually** has a shower in the morning.
often:     I **often** get up late at the weekend.
sometimes: I **sometimes** get home at 1.00 a.m.
0%  never: She **never** has dinner at home.

**Look!** Adverbs of frequency come after the verb *be*: We're **always** together on Sunday.

**Go to Grammar practice:** adverbs of frequency, page 99

**5 A** ▶4.4 **Pronunciation:** sentence stress  Listen to the sentences. Are the adverbs of frequency stressed or unstressed?

1  I usually get up at 7.00 a.m.
2  I always have a coffee for breakfast.
3  I never go to the gym.
4  I often make dinner in the evening.

**B** Listen again, check and repeat.

**6** Change the adverbs of frequency in 5A so the sentences are true for you.
In pairs, say the sentences with the correct stress.

A  *I sometimes get up at 7.00 a.m.*    B  *Really? I never get up at 7.00 a.m.*

**7 A** Look at the table. Write five sentences about Sally and Ashley's brother, Marcus.
*He always has breakfast in a café.*

|   | Mon | Tue | Wed | Thu | Fri |
|---|---|---|---|---|---|
| 1 have breakfast in a café | ✓ | ✓ | ✓ | ✓ | ✓ |
| 2 watch TV in the morning | ✓ | ✗ | ✓ | ✗ | ✓ |
| 3 work in the evening | ✓ | ✗ | ✓ | ✓ | ✓ |
| 4 see friends after work | ✗ | ✗ | ✗ | ✗ | ✓ |
| 5 go to bed before midnight | ✗ | ✗ | ✗ | ✗ | ✗ |

**B** ▶4.5  Listen and check. What is Marcus's job?

**Go to Communication practice:** Student A page 136, Student B page 144

**8** In pairs, compare yourself with members of your family. Use the activities in the boxes.
*I always get up before 7.00 a.m., but my brother usually gets up late, at 9.30.*

> get up before 7.00 a.m.   eat fast food   watch TV in the morning   go to bed late
>
> get home before 6.00 p.m.   have coffee for breakfast   have lunch at work   have a shower in the morning

**Personal Best**  Describe your typical daily routine at the weekend.

33

# 4 SKILLS

**READING** finding specific information ■ 's: possession or contraction ■ transport

## 4B My journey to work

**1** Match the types of transport with pictures a–e on page 35.

1  bike   _____
2  taxi   _____
3  bus    _____
4  car    _____
5  subway _____

**Go to Vocabulary practice:** transport, page 115

**2** Look at the pictures and the title of the text on page 35. Guess the answers to the questions. Read the text quickly and check.

1  What city is it about?
2  What type of transport is it about?

### Skill   finding specific information

**We sometimes need to find specific information in a text.**
- Read the questions carefully to see what information you need to find.
- Find the place in the text which has this information and read it carefully.
- Don't worry if you don't understand every word.

**3 A** Read the Skill box. Then find information in the paragraph about Emily in the text to complete the first line of the table.

|        | Lives where? | Which job? | Works where? |
|--------|--------------|------------|--------------|
| Emily  | *Harlem*     |            |              |
| Dan    |              |            |              |
| Megan  |              |            |              |
| Walter |              |            |              |

**B** Now find the information about the other people in the text. Complete the table.

**4** Read the text again. Then in pairs, say why each person uses a *citibike*.

*Emily uses a citibike because it's fast.*

**5** Complete the sentences from the text. In which sentences does 's mean *is*?

1  _____ office is in Downtown Manhattan.
2  'The _____ cheap,' she says.

### Text builder   's: possession or contraction

If you see 's at the end of a word, decide if it refers to possession or if it is a contraction of *is*.
The **city's** blue public bikes = **possession** (the bikes belong to the city)
**Megan's** a waitress in the Lower East Side = **contraction** (Megan is a waitress)

**6** Read the Text builder. Then read the sentences and write *P* (possession) or *C* (contraction).

1  Ravi's a doctor.                      _____
2  David's mum is a teacher.             _____
3  My train's always late.               _____
4  Julia's brother starts work at 7.00.  _____

**7** Discuss the questions in pairs.

1  Do you have public bikes in your town or city? Are they popular? Why/Why not?
2  How do you usually travel to work or university?
3  Do you like the journey? Why/Why not?

finding specific information ■ 's: possession or contraction ■ transport   READING   SKILLS   4B

# A morning in the life of bike 0827

New York is famous for its yellow taxis and noisy subway, but a lot of people also travel by *citibike* – the city's blue public bikes. New Yorkers make 14 million journeys a year on *citibikes*. Who uses them and why? We follow one bike for a morning to find out.

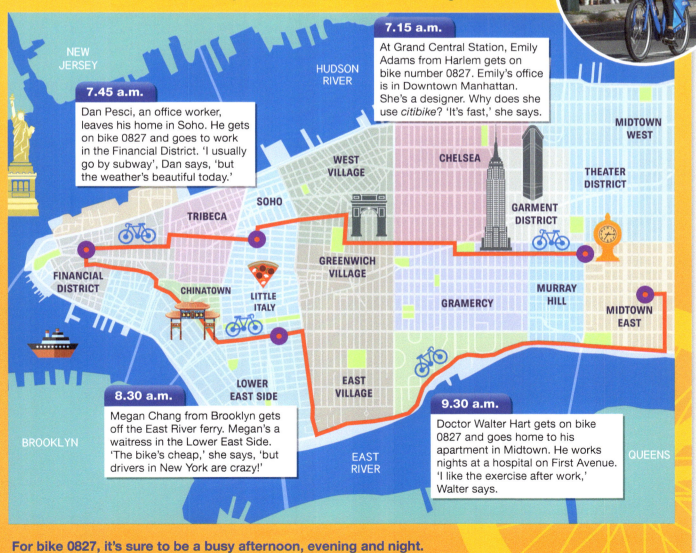

**7.15 a.m.**
At Grand Central Station, Emily Adams from Harlem gets on bike number 0827. Emily's office is in Downtown Manhattan. She's a designer. Why does she use *citibike*? 'It's fast,' she says.

**7.45 a.m.**
Dan Pesci, an office worker, leaves his home in Soho. He gets on bike 0827 and goes to work in the Financial District. 'I usually go by subway', Dan says, 'but the weather's beautiful today.'

**8.30 a.m.**
Megan Chang from Brooklyn gets off the East River ferry. Megan's a waitress in the Lower East Side. 'The bike's cheap,' she says, 'but drivers in New York are crazy!'

**9.30 a.m.**
Doctor Walter Hart gets on bike 0827 and goes home to his apartment in Midtown. He works nights at a hospital on First Avenue. 'I like the exercise after work,' Walter says.

For bike 0827, it's sure to be a busy afternoon, evening and night.

**Personal Best** Write about the different types of transport in your town or city.

# 4 LANGUAGE    present simple: *wh-* questions ■ adjectives (2)

## 4C  Where do you work?

**1** Match the adjectives in the box with their opposites.

> quiet   clean   hot   fast   unfriendly

1 dirty / _____  2 cold / _____  3 friendly / _____  4 noisy / _____  5 slow / _____

Go to Vocabulary practice: adjectives (2), page 116

**2 A** Write down two examples for each of these things.

> a cold country   a large building in your country   a noisy job   a long river   a fast animal
>
> a friendly café or shop in your town or city   a hot drink   a quiet place in your town or city

**B** Compare your answers in pairs. Do you have the same things?

**3** Read the text quickly and answer the questions.

1 What is Tess's job?  _____   3 What time does she start work?  _____
2 Does she like her job?  _____   4 Where does she live?  _____

# A Dirty Job?

 Tess Mitchell is a refuse collector. It's dirty work and she gets up very early, but she loves her job.

**What time do you start work?**
I start work at 5.00 in the morning. I get up at 4.15 a.m. and have breakfast. Then I leave for work.

**¹_____ do you work?**
I work in south London. The refuse centre isn't far from my house.

**²_____ do you do on a typical day?**
I drive the lorry to about 800 houses every day from Monday to Friday. That's a lot of rubbish!

**³_____ do you like the job?**
Because the people are friendly and I work outside. Sometimes it's very cold early in the morning, but when the weather's nice, I love it.

**⁴_____ do you finish work?**
I finish at 1.30 p.m. I'm a mum, so the hours are great. I get home at 2.00, have a shower, and then I go to my children's school to collect them.

**⁵_____ do you relax when you're not at work?**
I play football with a women's football team and we train on Tuesday and Thursday evenings. At the weekend, I get up late!

present simple: *wh-* questions ■ adjectives (2)     LANGUAGE  4C

**4** **A** Complete the questions in the text with the question words in the box. How do you say them in your language?

> Why   Where   When   What   How

**B** Look at the questions in the text again. Order the words below from 1–4 to make a question. Then read the Grammar box.

☐ *do/does*   ☐ main verb   ☐ question word   ☐ subject

📖 **Grammar**   present simple: *wh-* questions

| Question word: | *do/does*: | Subject: | Main verb: |
|---|---|---|---|
| Where | do | you | live? |
| What | does | your husband | do? |
| How | does | he | get to work? |
| When | do | your children | watch TV? |
| What time | do | they | get up? |
| Why | do | you | work at the weekend? |
| Who | do | you | work with? |

Go to Grammar practice: present simple: *wh-* questions, page 99

**5** ▶ 4.10 **Pronunciation: question words** Listen and repeat the question words. Do they begin with a /w/ sound or a /h/ sound?

1 where ____  2 when ____  3 who ____  4 why ____  5 how ____  6 what ____

**6 A** ▶ 4.11 Order the words to make questions. Say the questions with the correct pronunciation of the question words. Listen, check and repeat.

1 you / have / how many / do / children   _____ ?
2 what / they / time / have breakfast / do   _____ ?
3 do / does / husband / your / what   _____ ?
4 he / when / does / work   _____ ?
5 at the weekend / you / what / do / do   _____ ?

**B** ▶ 4.12 Match questions 1–5 with answers a–e. Listen to the interview with Tess and check.

a In the afternoons and evenings.
b Two.
c He's a taxi driver.
d 7.30.
e We often go to the park.

Go to Communication practice: Student A page 137, Student B page 145

**7 A** Find out about your partner. Ask and answer the questions in the boxes in pairs.

> What time / start work?   Who / live with?   How / get to English classes?
> What / have for breakfast?   Where / usually go on holiday?   How / relax in the evening?
> Why / study English?   When / do your English homework?   How many brothers and sisters / have?

**B** Swap partners. Ask and answer questions about your first partner.

A *What time does Sasha start work?*   B *He usually starts work at 8.00 a.m.*

**Personal Best**   Write ten questions for an interview with an actor/singer that you like.   37

# 4 SKILLS  SPEAKING   being polite in shops ■ shopping for food

## 4D  How can I help you?

**1 A** ▶ 4.13  Match the prices with the words. Listen and check.

1 nine euros ninety-nine  ____
2 nineteen pounds ninety-nine  ____
3 fifteen euros  ____
4 fifty dollars  ____
5 eleven dollars ninety-nine  ____
6 twenty-nine euros  ____
7 fifty pence/fifty p  ____
8 five pounds  ____
9 six pounds fifty  ____
10 fifty cents  ____
11 five pounds ninety-five  ____
12 twenty-five dollars  ____

**B** Write down three prices in numbers and give them to your partner. Say your partner's prices.

*That's three pounds fifty.*

**2** Discuss the questions in pairs.
1 Who usually goes shopping for food in your house?
2 Where do you usually buy food? Why?
   a at a supermarket   b at a market   c at local shops
3 Do you like shopping for food? Why/Why not?

Penny

**3** ▶ 4.14  Watch or listen to the first part of *Learning Curve*. Are the sentences true (T) or false (F)?
1 Penny likes shopping for food.  ____
2 Penny and Taylor live together.  ____
3 They usually go shopping on Thursdays.  ____
4 There is a big supermarket near their apartment.  ____

**4** ▶ 4.15  Watch or listen to the second part of the show. Tick (✓) the things Penny buys and the correct prices.

| shop 1 | shop 2 | shop 3 |
|---|---|---|
| half a chicken ☐ | cheese and salad ☐ | a blue shopping trolley ☐ |
| a whole chicken ☐ | cheese and eggs ☐ | a black shopping trolley ☐ |
| $4.79 ☐ | $17.15 ☐ | $21.77 ☐ |
| $8.79 ☐ | $17.50 ☐ | $22.02 ☐ |

**5** ▶ 4.15  Who says the phrases: Penny (P), Shop assistant 1 (S1), Shop assistant 2 (S2) or Shop assistant 3 (S3)? Watch or listen again and check.

1 How much is it for that small shopping trolley? ____
2 Here you are. ____
3 I'd like a whole chicken, please. ____
4 You're welcome. ____
5 Here's your change – 25 cents. ____
6 Can I have two pounds of this white cheese? ____

being polite in shops ■ shopping for food   **SPEAKING**   **SKILLS**   **4D**

### Conversation builder | shopping for food

**Customer:**
Do you have …?
Can I have …
I'd like …
How much is that?
Here you go/are.

**Shop assistant:**
How can I help you?
Anything else?
That's … dollars/pounds.
Here you go/are.
Here's your change.

**6 A** Read the Conversation builder. Then order the sentences from 1–7 to make a conversation in a shop.

a ☐ Yes. Anything else?
b ☐ Yes, I'd like five biscuits, please. How much is that?
c ☐ Can I have a chocolate cake, please?
d ☐ Thanks. And here's your change.
e ☐ Here you go – £10.
f ☐ Hello. How can I help you?
g ☐ That's £8.50.

**B** ▶ 4.16 Listen and check. Practise the conversation in pairs.

**7** ▶ 4.17 Complete the conversation with the words in the box. Listen and check. Are Penny and the shop assistant polite? Why/Why not?

welcome   good   thank you   please

**Shop assistant** ¹_____ evening.
**Penny** I'd like a whole chicken, ²_____ .
**Shop assistant** Here you go.

**Penny** ³_____ .
**Shop assistant** You're ⁴_____ .

### 🔧 Skill | being polite in shops

It's important to be polite if you work in a shop or if you're a customer.
• Greet people. Say: *Hi / Good morning / Good evening*, etc.
• Ask for things politely. Say: *Can I have …? / I'd like …, please.* NOT ~~I want … / Give me …~~
• If someone says: *Thanks / Thank you*, you can reply: *You're welcome. / That's alright.*

**8** ▶ 4.18 Read the Skill box. Listen to three conversations. Tick (✓) the people who are polite.

1 a the customer ☐   b the waiter ☐   c both people ☐
2 a the customer ☐   b the shop assistant ☐   c both people ☐
3 a the customer ☐   b the receptionist ☐   c both people ☐

**Go to Communication practice:** Student A page 137, Student B page 145

**9 A PREPARE** In pairs, look at the pictures and choose one of the situations. Write down things you can buy there and their prices.

In a burger restaurant

In a fruit and vegetable shop

In a café

**B PRACTISE** Decide who is the customer and who is the assistant. Act out your conversation.

**C PERSONAL BEST** Listen to another pair's conversation. Are they polite? What could they do better?

**Personal Best** Think of your favourite food shop or café and write a conversation in English there.

# 3 and 4 REVIEW and PRACTICE

## Grammar

**1** Tick (✓) the correct sentences.

1. a  I never finish work at 5.00 p.m.
   b  I don't never finish work at 5.00 p.m.
   c  I don't finish work never at 5.00 p.m.
2. a  He don't go to bed early.
   b  He not go to bed early.
   c  He doesn't go to bed early.
3. a  Do you go to work by car?
   b  Does you go to work by car?
   c  When you do go to work by car?
4. a  We often has eggs for breakfast.
   b  We often have eggs for breakfast.
   c  We have often eggs for breakfast.
5. a  Why do you live with?
   b  Who do you live with?
   c  How do you live with?
6. a  When they do get up?
   b  When they get up?
   c  When do they get up?
7. a  She work in a restaurant in the evening.
   b  She do work in a restaurant in the evening.
   c  She works in a restaurant in the evening.
8. a  Goes he to the gym after work?
   b  Does he to the gym after work?
   c  Does he go to the gym after work?

**2** Order the words to make questions and sentences.

1. your / do / go / children / where / school / to
   _____?
2. have / she / at / does / lunch / home
   _____?
3. always / dinner / we / eat / vegetables / for
   _____.
4. get / time / what / weekend / do / up / the / you / at
   _____?
5. don't / shopping / I / Saturday / go / on
   _____.
6. the / he / book / sometimes / a / reads / train / on
   _____.
7. Monday / quiet / restaurant / is / on / often / the
   _____.
8. in / radio / do / listen / to / you / the / morning / the
   _____?
9. old / brother's / is / how / your / girlfriend
   _____?
10. the / never / exercise / Simon / weekend / does / at
    _____.

**3** Complete the text with the correct form of the verbs in brackets.

# Life on Muck

 This is Laura Marriner. She lives and works on the very small island of Muck in Scotland. Life isn't easy, but it's very interesting …

**What** ¹_____ (be) Laura's job?
She's a teacher. Her school only ²_____ (have) eight children.

**Where** ³_____ she _____ (live)?
Laura ⁴_____ (not leave) home in the morning because she lives in the school with her husband and two sons!

**How** ⁵_____ they _____ (go) shopping?
By ferry. The journey is two hours, but people on the island only ⁶_____ (use) the ferry when the weather is good. They ⁷_____ (not go) shopping every day, so Laura ⁸_____ (make) bread at home.

**What is school life like on Muck?**
It's great. The children often ⁹_____ (study) on the beach.

¹⁰_____ Laura _____ (like) life on Muck?
Yes, she does! When the weather is horrible, life is difficult, but she's happy there. The people are very friendly and life is an adventure.

## Vocabulary

**1** Put the words in the box in the correct columns.

| ~~boat~~ ~~cold~~ ~~do~~ cheese fast finish get up |
| know small meat noisy short taxi train want |

| Verbs | Adjectives | Nouns |
|---|---|---|
| do | cold | boat |

40

REVIEW and PRACTICE  3 and 4

**2** Circle the word that is different. Explain your answers.

| 1 | car | lorry | bus | plane |
| 2 | think | use | slow | make |
| 3 | Friday | tomorrow | Sunday | Saturday |
| 4 | rice | chips | crisps | potatoes |
| 5 | coffee | milk | fruit | orange juice |
| 6 | clean | horrible | unfriendly | dirty |
| 7 | biscuit | pizza | cake | chocolate |
| 8 | work | study | change | dinner |

**3** Complete the sentences with the correct words.

1 What time do you g_et_ home after work?
2 He usually l_____ to the radio at work.
3 I always have b_____ before I leave home in the morning.
4 They w_____ television after dinner.
5 She goes to university by m_____ . It's very fast.
6 In cold weather, I have a h_____ drink in the evening.
7 He never says 'hello'. He's so u_____ .
8 T_____ in New York are yellow and in London they're black.
9 I never drink tea, coffee or soft drinks. I only drink w_____ with meals.
10 On W_____ evening, I go to the gym.

**4** Complete the email with the words in the box.

bike  dressed  bread  friendly  get  live
go  evening  Saturday  read

Hi Ana,

How are you? I'm in Cartagena at my grandmother's house this week. It's nice and quiet here. I ¹_____ up late every day, have breakfast and get ²_____ . Then I go to the shops by ³_____ . I usually buy some ⁴_____ for lunch. The people are very ⁵_____ . In the afternoon, I ⁶_____ to the beach and ⁷_____ a book. In the ⁸_____ , we sometimes have dinner in a restaurant.

I'm here for one week, and then I go home on ⁹_____ ☹ ... I want to ¹⁰_____ here!

See you soon.

Bea

## Personal Best

**Lesson 3A** — Name four things people eat or drink for breakfast.

**Lesson 4A** — Write four sentences about your daily routine with adverbs of frequency.

**Lesson 3A** — Write a sentence about the food you like and don't like.

**Lesson 4B** — Name six types of transport.

**Lesson 3B** — Name the days of the week that begin with 'T'.

**Lesson 4B** — Describe a member of your family's bike, car or motorbike.

**Lesson 3B** — Write a sentence about something you do every week.

**Lesson 4C** — Write three adjectives that describe your town or city.

**Lesson 3C** — Write a positive and a negative sentence about a friend's typical day.

**Lesson 4C** — Write three questions for your teacher with different question words.

**Lesson 3D** — Write about the food you eat on a special occasion. Use *and* and *but*.

**Lesson 4D** — Write a sentence to ask for something to eat and drink in a café.

41

# UNIT 5

# All about me

**LANGUAGE**  *can* and *can't* ■ common verbs (2)

## 5A When can you start?

**1** Complete phrases 1–5 with the verbs in the box.

swim   speak   drive   play   call

1 _____ a car   2 _____ Chinese   3 _____ the piano   4 _____ a friend   5 _____ in the sea

Go to Vocabulary practice: common verbs (2), page 117

**2** Read the job advert. What do you need for this job?

**SYDNEY CITY TOURS: TOUR GUIDE**

Help tourists see the beautiful city of Sydney.

Do you know Sydney? Do you like working with people? Can you speak a foreign language? Do you want to work this summer?

If the answer is 'Yes', then contact us.   ▶ CONTACT

**3** ▶5.2 Listen to a job interview. Tick (✓) the things Georgia can do. Does she get the job?

|   | Yes | No |
|---|---|---|
| 1 Can you speak a foreign language? |  |  |
| 2 Can you drive? |  |  |
| 3 Can you work early in the morning? |  |  |
| 4 Can you swim well? |  |  |

**4 A** ▶5.2 Match the halves to make sentences. Listen again and check.

1 Some of the people can't         a can.
2 I can speak                       b start?
3 Yes, I                            c Chinese.
4 No, I                             d can't – sorry.
5 When can you                      e speak English.

**B** Choose the correct options to complete the rules. Then read the Grammar box.

1 We use *can* to talk about *abilities / daily routines*.
2 We use *can't* + verb in *questions / negatives*.
3 We use *can* + subject + verb in *questions / negatives*.

42

*can* and *can't* ■ common verbs (2)   **LANGUAGE**   **5A**

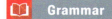 **Grammar** *can* and *can't*

Positive:
I **can work** this summer.
Georgia **can swim** well.

Negative:
I **can't speak** Chinese.
They **can't cook**.

Questions and short answers:
**Can** you **speak** a foreign language?
Yes, I **can**.   No, I **can't**.

Go to Grammar practice: *can* and *can't*, page 100

**5** ▶5.4 **Pronunciation:** *can* and *can't* Listen and repeat. Pay attention to the difference between *can* /kæn/ or /kən/ and *can't* /kɑːnt/.

1  He can drive.    2  She can't swim.    3  Can you play the guitar?    4  Yes, I can.

**6 A** ▶5.5 Say the sentences with the correct pronunciation of *can* and *can't*. Listen, check and repeat.

1  I can swim two kilometres.    3  I can't speak German.    5  I can drive a car.
2  I can't sing well.              4  I can cook Italian food.   6  I can't play the piano.

**B** Say the sentences in pairs. Say if you think it's true or false for your partner.

A  *I can swim two kilometres.*    B  *False. You can't swim two kilometres.*
A  *You're right, I can't swim.*

**7 A** Read the job advert. What does an *au pair* do?

**B** ▶5.6 Emily and Ben are interested in the job. Listen and tick (✓) what they can and can't do.

### AU PAIR
- Can you look after children?
- Do you like sports and music?
- Do you want to work as an au pair this summer?

We're a friendly American family with two children. We live in Madrid, Spain.

– *Contact Lisa Jones for more information.* –

| Can he/she … | Emily | Ben |
|---|---|---|
| cook? | | |
| drive? | | |
| speak Spanish? | | |
| play tennis? | | |
| swim? | | |
| play the piano? | | |
| play the guitar? | | |

**8** ▶5.7 In pairs, ask and answer the questions about Emily and Ben. Who is best for the job? Listen and check.

A  *Can Emily cook?*    B  *Yes, she can.*

Go to Communication practice: Student A page 137, Student B page 145

**9 A** Ask your classmates questions 1–5. Find someone who says 'Yes, I can.' and write his/her name. Then ask for more information.

A  *Can you speak a foreign language?*    B  *Yes, I can.*
A  *Which language can you speak?*         B  *I can speak French.*

| Questions | Name | More information |
|---|---|---|
| 1  Can you speak a foreign language? | | |
| 2  Can you play an instrument? | | |
| 3  Can you dance? | | |
| 4  Can you cook? | | |
| 5  Can you play a sport? | | |

**B** In pairs, discuss what you found out about your classmates.

*Sebastian can speak French.*

**Personal Best**  Write ten sentences about people in your class. Use *can* and *can't*.

43

# 5 SKILLS  LISTENING — listening for specific information ■ sentence stress ■ electronic devices

## 5B I can't live without my phone

**1** Match the words in the box with the electronic devices 1–6. Is your family like this?

headphones   laptop   smartphone   MP3 player   TV   remote control

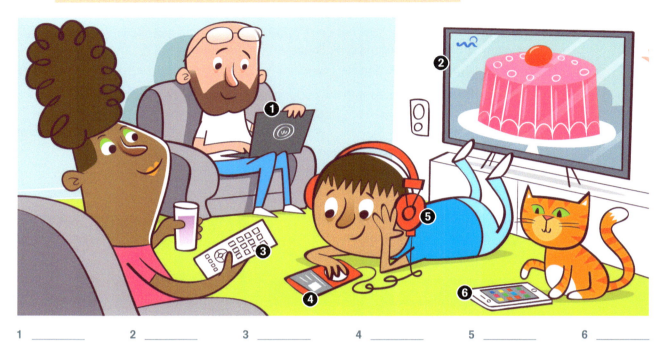

1 _____   2 _____   3 _____   4 _____   5 _____   6 _____

**Go to Vocabulary practice:** electronic devices, page 118

**2** Which electronic devices do you have? Discuss in pairs.
*I have a laptop, but I don't have a tablet.*

**3** ▶ 5.9   Watch or listen to the first part of *Learning Curve*. Tick (✓) the devices Kate mentions.
camera ☐   desktop computer ☐   TV ☐   smartphone ☐   laptop ☐   headphones ☐

### 🔧 Skill   listening for specific information

We sometimes need to listen for specific information.
• Read the questions to find out what information you need.
• Think about the topic and what type of information it is, e.g. a person, a place, a number, etc.
• Listen carefully when the speakers talk about this topic.

**4** ▶ 5.9   Read the Skill box. Watch or listen again and choose the correct options to answer the questions.
1 Which sport does Kate do on Friday?
   a basketball   b football   c tennis
2 What language does she learn on her tablet and phone?
   a Spanish   b French   c Italian
3 What device can't she live without?
   a tablet   b camera   c phone
4 How many photos do people take every year?
   a one million   b one billion   c one trillion
5 How many televisions do people in the USA have?
   a 116 million   b 123 million   c 26 million

44

listening for specific information ■ sentence stress ■ electronic devices  **LISTENING**  SKILLS  **5B**

**5** ▶ 5.10  Watch or listen to the rest of the show. Complete the sentences with the words in the box.

headphones   DVR   car   laptop   tablet   music

1 Simon can't live without _____ or his _____ .

2 Parminder can't live without her _____ and _____ .

3 Vincent can't live without his _____ and his _____ .

**6** ▶ 5.10  Watch or listen again. Choose the correct options to complete the sentences.

1 Parminder uses her devices for *presentations* / *letters* / *games*.
2 She uses her devices *at the weekend* / *at night* / *every day*.
3 Vincent can play *the piano* / *the violin* / *the guitar*.
4 His car is from *1962* / *1967* / *1972*.
5 Simon travels *by underground* / *on foot* / *by car*.

**7** ▶ 5.11  Listen to Vincent's sentence. Is it easy to hear the underlined words? Why?

> And when I <u>get</u> <u>home</u>, I <u>watch</u> <u>TV</u> at <u>night</u>.

**Listening builder** | **sentence stress**

In English, we stress the important words in sentences. You can usually understand the general idea if you only hear these words.
I <u>play</u> <u>basketball</u> on <u>Fridays</u> with a <u>women's</u> <u>team</u>.
I <u>work</u> for a <u>big</u> <u>company</u> and we <u>use</u> <u>all</u> the <u>top</u> <u>technology</u>.

**8 A** ▶ 5.12  Read the Listening builder. Read and listen to sentences 1–4. Can you understand them?

1 _____ can't live without _____ phone. _____ _____ call people _____ take photos.
2 _____ brother's _____ doctor. _____ usually goes _____ _____ hospital _____ car.
3 Kevin wants _____ new laptop, _____ _____ very expensive.
4 _____ _____ morning, _____ always listen _____ _____ radio.

**B** ▶ 5.12  Listen again and complete the sentences with the unstressed words.

**9** In pairs, talk about your electronic devices. Answer the questions.

1 What do you use your devices for?
2 Which device can't you live without? Why not?

A *I use my phone to listen to music and take photos. What about you?*
B *I don't use my phone to listen to music. I have an MP3 player.*

**Personal Best**  Write about your favourite electronic device. Say when and where you use it.

45

# 5 LANGUAGE    object pronouns ■ activities

## 5C I love it!

**1** Match the words in the box with pictures a–f.

cycling   walking   cleaning   swimming   reading   cooking

**Go to Vocabulary practice:** activities, page 119

**2 A** Write two activities in each column.

| 😊 I love … | 😄 I like … | 🙁 I don't like … | 😔 I hate … |
|---|---|---|---|
|  |  |  |  |

**B** Tell your partner about what you love, like, don't like and hate.

**A** *I love cooking.*   **B** *Really? I hate cooking. I love going out!*

**3 A** Look at the pictures on the webpage. What activities can you see?

**B** Read the text. Complete the sentences with *loves*, *likes*, *doesn't like* and *hates*.

1  Midori _____ listening to music. She _____ Adele.
2  Laura _____ shopping for food.
3  Diego _____ his grandad.
4  Josh _____ sleeping late because he _____ early mornings.
5  Ellie _____ watching movies with her friends and she _____ popcorn.

## That's ⓘnteresting    LIKES AND DISLIKES

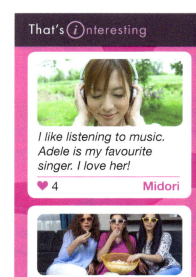

*I like listening to music. Adele is my favourite singer. I love her!*

♥ 4    **Midori**

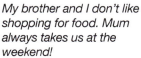

*I like watching movies with my friends. We always have a big bowl of popcorn – I love it!*

♥ 6    **Ellie**

*My brother and I don't like shopping for food. Mum always takes us at the weekend!*

♥ 7    **Laura**

*I love my grandad. I can always talk to him and he helps me a lot.*

♥ 12    **Diego**

*I love sleeping late at weekends. Early mornings? I hate them!*

♥ 3    **Josh**

object pronouns ■ activities

LANGUAGE 5C

**4** **A** Match the object pronouns in **bold** with the people and things. Read the text again and check.

1  I love **her**!
2  Mum always takes **us** at the weekend!
3  I can always talk to **him**.
4  He helps **me** a lot.
5  I hate **them**!
6  I love **it**!

a  Diego
b  early mornings
c  Adele
d  popcorn
e  Laura and her brother
f  Diego's grandad

**B** Choose the correct words to complete the sentences. Then read the Grammar box.

1  We use object pronouns instead of *people and things / times and places*.
2  We use object pronouns *before / after* verbs.

### Grammar    object pronouns

| Subject pronouns: | Object pronouns: | |
|---|---|---|
| I | me | *I don't understand. Can you help **me**?* |
| you | you | *Are **you** Adam? This is for **you**.* |
| he | him | *He isn't friendly. I don't like **him**.* |
| she | her | *She works in your office. Do you know **her**?* |
| it | it | *It's perfect. I love **it**!* |
| we | us | *We're in the garden. Can you see **us**?* |
| they | them | *They're new here. I don't know **them**.* |

Go to Grammar practice: object pronouns, page 100

**5** **A** ▶ 5.15 **Pronunciation:** /h/ Listen and repeat. Pay attention to the sound /h/.

him    her    he    help    happy

**B** ▶ 5.16 Say the questions and sentences. Then listen, check and repeat.

1  Do you like him?    2  I can't see her.    3  He hates horses.    4  Hi, Harry. How are you?

**6** ▶ 5.17 Complete the conversation with object pronouns. Listen and check.

A  Do you like Emma Stone?
B  Yes, I do. I love ¹_____ . She's great!
A  What about Bruno Mars?
B  Yes, I like ²_____ too.
A  Do you like shopping for clothes?

B  No, I hate ³_____ .
A  Do you like Monday mornings?
B  No, I hate ⁴_____ .
A  What do you think of cats?
B  I don't like ⁵_____ , but they like ⁶_____ !

Go to Communication practice: Student A page 138, Student B page 146

**7** **A** Write three examples in each of the circles.

singers and bands    actors    food and drink    animals    activities

**B** In pairs, ask and answer questions about the people and things.

Do you like …?    What about …?    What do you think of …?

**8** Tell the class about you and your partner.

*We both love cats. I like Ryan Gosling, but Carla doesn't like him.*

**Personal Best**    Write a conversation like the one in exercise 6 between you and someone in your family.

47

# 5 SKILLS    WRITING describing yourself ■ because

## 5D My profile

**1 A** Look at the profile on the 'CityMeet' app. What do you think you can do with the app?
  a  find an apartment in a city    b  make new friends in a city    c  find a new job in a city
  **B** Read the profile and check.

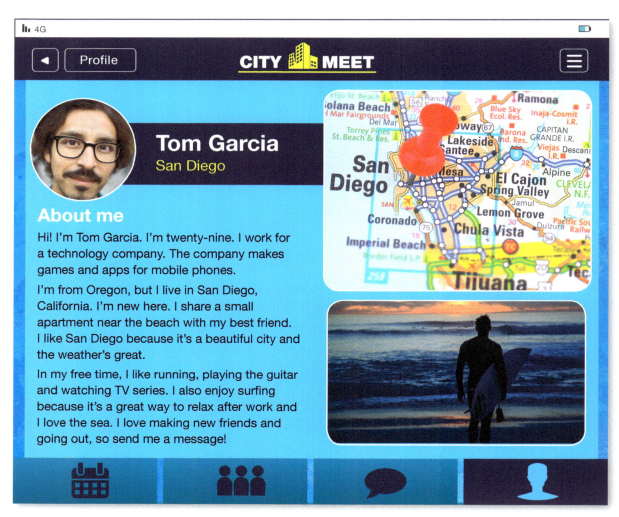

**2** Read the profile again. Complete the sentences with the correct words.
  1  Tom works for a _____ company.
  2  He's from _____ , but he lives in _____ .
  3  He lives near the _____ with his _____ .
  4  He thinks the weather in San Diego is _____ .
  5  He plays the _____ and watches _____ in his free time.
  6  He loves making _____ .

> **Skill** describing yourself
>
> **When you write a text to describe yourself, use a different paragraph for each topic.**
> • personal information about you and your job: *Hi! My name's Fiona. I'm a teacher.*
> • where you live: *I live in York. I share a flat with my best friend.*
> • what you do in your free time: *In my free time, I like listening to music and cooking for friends.*
> • information about your family: *I have a brother. His name's Paul and he's 18.*

**3** Read the Skill box. Tick (✓) the topics which are in Tom's profile.
  a  his job ☐      b  where he lives ☐      c  his family ☐      d  his free-time activities ☐

48

describing yourself ■ *because* **WRITING** **SKILLS** **5D**

**4** Complete Kimberley's profile with sentences a–c.
  a I also love travelling because it's a great way to meet new people.
  b I study French and Spanish. I can also speak Portuguese.
  c We love San Diego because it's a fun and exciting city.

**ABOUT ME**

Hello! I'm Kimberley Watson and I'm a student at the University of San Diego. ¹____
I live in a house with four friends. We're all students. ²____
In my free time, I like watching French films, running and going out with my friends. ³____

**5** Imagine Tom and Kimberley meet on CityMeet. Do they become friends? Choose an option and complete the sentence.

Tom and Kimberley *become / don't become* friends because _____ .

**Text builder** | *because*

We use *because* to give a reason. It answers the question *Why?*
*I like San Diego **because** it's a beautiful city.*
*Why do you like travelling?* **Because** *it's a great way to meet new people.*

**6 A** Read the Text builder and find sentences with *because* in Tom and Kimberley's profiles. How do you say *because* in your language?

**B** Match 1–5 with a–e. Make sentences with *because*.

1 I live in a small flat          a I'm usually tired after work.
2 I go to work by bus             b it's good exercise.
3 I like swimming                 c it's quiet and the people are friendly.
4 I don't often go to the gym     d houses in my city are expensive.
5 I like living in a village      e I can't drive.

**7** Complete the sentences with your own ideas.
  1 I love my city/town because _____ .
  2 I'm often tired in the evening because _____ .
  3 I like cooking because _____ .
  4 I don't often go out because _____ .
  5 I usually get up early because _____ .

**8 A** **PREPARE** Plan an online profile for you. Decide what information to include. Make notes about:
  • your personal information
  • your work or study
  • where you live and who you live with
  • your free-time activities and why you like them

**B** **PRACTISE** Write your profile. Use one paragraph for each topic. Remember to use *because* to give reasons.

**C** **PERSONAL BEST** Read your partner's profile. Does each paragraph contain one topic? Choose a paragraph that you like and tell your partner why you like it.

**Personal Best** Write a profile of a friend or someone in your family.

# UNIT 6

## Places

**LANGUAGE**  there is/are ■ places in a town

### 6A City or village?

1 Match the words in the box with places 1–6.

| bank | bus stop | restaurant |
| hotel | supermarket | post office |

1 _____  3 _____  5 _____
2 _____  4 _____  6 _____

Go to Vocabulary practice: places in a town, page 120

2 **A** Look at the pictures of Whycocomagh in Canada. Is it a city, town or village?

**B** Read the text and tick (✓) the things Whycocomagh has.

1 shopping centre ☐    3 cinema ☐    5 school ☐
2 supermarket ☐        4 nightclub ☐  6 restaurants ☐

## An unusual job offer

Whycocomagh is a small village on the beautiful island of Cape Breton in Canada, but the local supermarket has a problem. It needs three new shop assistants and people don't want to come to live in Whycocomagh because it's very quiet and far from any big cities.

So the owners of the Farmer's Daughter store put an unusual job advert on Facebook. It says, *'We can't give you big money, but we can give you an awesome life'* … and they offer over 8 km² of free land!

Thousands of people from around the world are interested and want to work in the village, so now the supermarket has some new shop assistants. But what's the village really like? We talk to Kelly Jenkins, a teacher at the village school.

**Tell us about Whycocomagh, Kelly.**
It's small, but it's beautiful. There's a school, a post office and the local supermarket, of course! There are also some hotels and restaurants for tourists.

**Is there a shopping centre or a cinema?**
No, there isn't! There aren't any big shops and there isn't a cinema or a nightclub. But there are some wonderful people here. Everyone is very friendly.

**Are there any problems?**
Yes, there are … but life's boring without any problems!

3 Complete the sentences with the words in the box. Check your answers in the text.

| isn't   's   aren't   are (x2)   is |

1 There _____ a school.
2 _____ there a shopping centre?
3 There _____ any big shops.
4 There _____ a cinema.
5 There _____ some wonderful people.
6 _____ there any problems?

50

*there is/are* ■ places in a town **LANGUAGE** **6A**

**4** Look at the sentences in exercise 3 again and choose the correct options to complete the rules. Then read the Grammar box.

1 We use *there's* and *there isn't* with *singular / plural* nouns.
2 We use *there are* and *there aren't* with *singular / plural* nouns.
3 We use *some / any* with plural nouns in positive sentences.
4 We use *some / any* with plural nouns in negative sentences and questions.

### Grammar — *there is/are*

| Positive: | Negative: | Questions: | Short answers: | |
|---|---|---|---|---|
| There's a cinema. | There isn't a museum. | Is there a park? | Yes, there is. | No, there isn't. |
| There are some shops. | There aren't any cafés. | Are there any hotels? | Yes, there are. | No, there aren't. |

Go to Grammar practice: *there is/are*, page 101

**5** In pairs, say if you want to live in Whycocomagh. Explain your answers.

*I don't want to live in Wycocomagh because there …*

**6** ▶ 6.3  Complete the text with the correct form of *there is/are*. Listen and check.

This is the beautiful city of Lavasa in India. [1]_____ some nice flats near the river. [2]_____ a post office, a police station and [3]_____ some great restaurants and cafés. [4]_____ a train station, but if you need to travel by train, you can take a taxi to Pune, which is 60 km away. However, [5]_____ something strange about Lavasa … nobody lives here! [6]_____ any people in the flats. At the weekends, [7]_____ some tourists in the restaurants and hotels, but they're on holiday.

**7 A** ▶ 6.4  **Pronunciation: linking consonants and vowels** Listen and repeat the sentences from exercise 6. Pay attention to how the sounds link together.

1 There's‿a post‿office.
2 There‿isn't‿a train station.
3 There‿aren't‿any people.
4 There‿are some tourists.

**B** ▶ 6.5  Say the sentences linking the sounds together. Listen, check and repeat.

1 There's‿a hospital.
2 Is there‿a bank?
3 There‿are some‿offices.
4 There‿aren't‿any museums.
5 There‿isn't‿a park.
6 Are there‿any schools?

Go to Communication practice: Student A page 138, Student B page 146

**8 A** ▶ 6.6  Listen to the conversation. Where does Erica live? Is she happy there?

**B** ▶ 6.6  Are the sentences about the area where Erica lives true (T) or false (F)? Listen again and check.

1 There's a big park. _____
2 There's a supermarket. _____
3 There aren't any shops. _____
4 There's a café in her street. _____
5 There isn't a bus stop near her house. _____
6 There are some good restaurants. _____

**9** Ask and answer the questions in pairs.

- Where do you live?
- Is it a city, a town or a village?
- What's your area like?
- Is there a …?
- Are there any …?

  Write about a city, town or village you know well.

51

# 6 SKILLS READING  reading in detail ■ giving opinions ■ parts of the body

## 6B City art

**1 A** Look at the pictures of public art on page 53. Do you like them? Why/Why not?

**B** Read the text quickly. In which cities can you see the three pieces of art?

**We sometimes have to read part of a text in detail to understand it well.**
- Read the question and find the paragraph of the text that has the information you need.
- Read the paragraph very carefully to answer the question.
- We sometimes use different words and phrases to give the same information.

**2** Read the Skill box. Chose the correct options to complete the sentences. Underline the phrase in the text that helped you answer the questions.

1 Carla and Mason have ____ .
   a jobs at the same hotel   b lots of cameras   c different opinions about *Eye*
2 Bruno Catalano ____ .
   a makes sculptures   b only has one arm   c is from Spain
3 Elodie and Christine ____ .
   a are friends of the artist   b live in Marseille   c are on holiday
4 Günther ____ the lifesaver sculpture.
   a likes   b doesn't like   c doesn't give an opinion about
5 Helga works ____ .
   a in a school   b in a restaurant   c as a taxi driver

**3** Match the words in the box with parts of the body 1–7 in the pictures on page 53.

| head  foot  eye  body  leg  hand  arm |

1 _____   2 _____   3 _____   4 _____   5 _____   6 _____   7 _____

**Go to Vocabulary practice:** parts of the body, page 121

**4** Match the people with the opinions.

1 Carla                    a 'I don't think it means anything.'
2 Mason                    b 'I like it.'
3 Elodie and Christine     c 'I think this is really ugly.'
4 Günther                  d 'In my opinion, that's what it means.'
5 Helga                    e 'It's beautiful.'

### Text builder — giving opinions

**Phrases:** *In my opinion, …   In my view, …*
**Verbs:** *I think/don't think …   I like/don't like …*
**Adjectives:** *It's beautiful/ugly/interesting/boring/strange*, etc.

**Look!** We say: *I don't think it's ugly.*
NOT ~~I think it isn't ugly.~~

**5** Read the Text builder. In pairs, describe the sculptures in the pictures and give your opinions.

a

b

c

reading in detail ■ giving opinions ■ parts of the body  **READING**  SKILLS  **6B**

# I love it ...
# but what is it?

There's art everywhere in our towns, cities and parks. Sometimes it's good, sometimes it's bad, but it's always interesting.

### Eye
In the garden of a five-star hotel in Dallas, USA, there's a 10-metre-high eye, called *Eye*. 'It's really interesting,' says Carla, a receptionist at the hotel. 'There are cameras everywhere today, watching us. In my opinion, that's what it means.' Mason, a waiter from another hotel, doesn't agree. 'I don't think it means anything,' he says. 'It's just an eye!'

### Travellers
In Marseille, France, there's an amazing sculpture by the French artist Bruno Catalano. It's a man on a journey. He only has one arm and he doesn't have a body. 'It's beautiful', say Elodie and her friend Christine, tourists from Paris.
'Perhaps it means that when we leave a place, we leave a part of us behind.'

### Lifesaver fountain
This fountain in Duisburg in Germany is big and colourful. It has a person's legs, but a bird's head and feet. But what is it? And what do local people think? 'I usually like modern art,' says Günther, a taxi driver. 'But I think this is really ugly.' Helga, a teacher, disagrees. 'I like it,' she says. 'I often have lunch in a restaurant on this street. When I see the fountain, I feel happy.'

**Personal Best**   Write about a piece of art you like and give your opinion of it.

53

# 6 LANGUAGE — prepositions of place ■ rooms and furniture

## 6C An unusual home

**1** Match the furniture in the box with pictures a–f.

fridge   table   bed   sofa   wardrobe   chair

a
b
c
d
e
f

**Go to Vocabulary practice:** rooms and furniture, page 122

**2** In pairs, describe a room in your house. Can your partner guess the room?

A *There's a table and four chairs in this room.*   B *Is it your kitchen?*
A *No, it's my living room!*

**3** Look at the picture. Guess where Kirsten lives. Read the text and check.

# Life on the water

For university students, a room in a flat or a house can be very expensive, but not for 20-year-old Kirsten Müller. Kirsten is a student at a business school in Berlin … and she lives on a boat! It's small, but it's home.
Kirsten is on the sofa in the living room. There's a small table in front of her. 'I study here every night,' she says. 'And I eat here too.' The kitchen has an electric cooker, and next to it, there's a small fridge. Kirsten cooks all her meals on the boat. 'It's perfect for me, but I can't invite lots of friends for dinner!' The bedroom has a bed … and nothing else! All of Kirsten's clothes are in boxes under the bed because there isn't a wardrobe. Between the bedroom and the kitchen, there's a modern bathroom with a shower and a toilet.
Kirsten loves her home. It's cheap and the people on the other boats are friendly, but are there any problems? 'I don't like getting up in winter,' she says. 'It's very cold!'

**4** Read the text again. Match the rooms in the box with the parts of the boat.

living room   bathroom   bedroom   kitchen

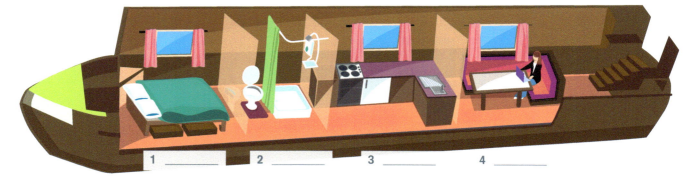

1 _____   2 _____   3 _____   4 _____

prepositions of place ■ rooms and furniture  **LANGUAGE  6C**

**5** Look at the diagram in exercise 4 again. Complete the sentences with the prepositions of place in the box. Check your answers in the text. Then read the Grammar box.

under   between   in   on   next to   in front of

1 Kirsten is _____ the sofa.
2 There's a small table _____ her.
3 The kitchen has an electric cooker, and _____ it, there's a small fridge.
4 All of Kirsten's clothes are _____ boxes _____ the bed.
5 _____ the bedroom and the kitchen, there's a modern bathroom.

### Grammar   prepositions of place

There's a table **next to** the sofa.
My mobile phone is **in** my bag.
Your shoes are **under** the bed.
My keys are **on** the table.

My bedroom is **above** our living room.
Luca sits **between** Carlos and Emma.
Your car is **in front of** our house.
The cat is **behind** the sofa.

Go to Grammar practice: prepositions of place, page 101

**6** ▶ 6.10 **Pronunciation:** sentence stress Listen and repeat the sentences. Pay attention to the underlined stressed words.

1 The camera is under my bed.
2 Your head is in front of the TV.
3 His shoes are next to the sofa.
4 The bathroom is behind the door.

**7 A** Complete the sentences with the correct prepositions of place.

1 The window is _____ the table.
2 Your keys are _____ the book.
3 The books are _____ the shelves.
4 There's a bed _____ the window and the chair.

**B** ▶ 6.11   In pairs, say the sentences with the correct stress. Listen, check and repeat.

**8 A** ▶ 6.12 Look at the picture and listen to the description. Find five differences between the description and the picture.

**B** ▶ 6.12 Compare your answers in pairs. Listen again and check.

*There isn't a clock on the table. There's a lamp on the table.*

Go to Communication practice: Student A page 138, Student B page 146

**9 A** Think of a room in your house. Make notes about what furniture is in it and where it is.

**B** In pairs, describe your room. Your partner draws it. Then check your pictures.

**10** Ask and answer the questions in pairs.

1 Do you live in a house or a flat?
2 Which is your favourite room? Why?
3 Imagine your ideal bedroom/living room/kitchen. What's in it?

**Personal Best**   Write about your 'dream' home.

# 6 SKILLS  SPEAKING  checking information ■ asking for and giving directions

## 6D Is there a post office near here?

**1** In pairs, discuss what you usually do when you're lost.
  a Ask someone in the street for directions.
  b Go into a shop and ask for directions.
  c Look at a map.
  d Use a Sat Nav app on your phone.
  e Walk around and hope you find the place.

**2** ▶ 6.13 Watch or listen to the first part of *Learning Curve*. Choose the correct words to complete the sentences.
  1 Simon has *cereal and tea / eggs, toast and coffee / eggs, toast and tea* for breakfast.
  2 He never goes to work *by car / by bike / on the underground*.
  3 Kate always says *'the underground' / 'the subway' / 'the tube'*.
  4 The man wants to find *a car park / a post office / the underground station*.

**3** ▶ 6.13 Complete the conversation with phrases a–e. Watch or listen again and check.

| | | | |
|---|---|---|---|
| **Man** | Excuse me. ¹_____ | a | It's on the left, near the car park. |
| **Simon** | Yes, there is. ²_____ | b | Thank you very much. |
| | Go straight on. ³_____ | c | No problem. |
| **Man** | ⁴_____ | d | It's down the street. |
| **Simon** | ⁵_____ | e | Is there a post office around here? |

### ✦ Conversation builder   asking for and giving directions

**Asking for directions:**
*Excuse me.*
*Is there a post office near here?*
*Is there a post office around here?*
*Where's the post office?*

**Giving directions:**
*Go straight on.*
*Go down this street.*
*Turn right/left at …*
*It's on the right/left/corner.*
*It's near/next to/in front of …*

**4 A** Read the Conversation builder. In pairs, look at the maps and ask for and give directions to the places in orange.

  **A** *Excuse me, where's the bank?*   **B** *Go straight on …*

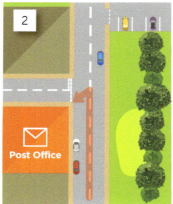

**B** ▶ 6.14 Listen and check. Are your conversations similar?

56

checking information ■ asking for and giving directions  **SPEAKING**  **SKILLS**  **6D**

**5** ▶ 6.15 Watch or listen to the second part of the show. Choose the correct options to answer the questions.

1 Where do the women want to go?
   a To the cinema.
   b To the shopping centre.
   c To the supermarket.

2 What's the problem at the studio?
   a There isn't any water.
   b There isn't any tea.
   c There isn't any electricity.

**6** ▶ 6.15 Watch or listen again. Complete the conversations with the phrases in the box.

a problem   show me   near here   did you say   repeat that   you mean

1 **Woman 1** Is there a shopping centre 1_____?
  **Simon** Yes, it's near the supermarket. Go down this street, turn right on Bethnal Green Road. Don't stop at Ebor Street. Go straight on.
  **Woman 2** Sorry, 2_____ near the supermarket?

2 **Woman 1** Can you 3_____ on the map?
  **Simon** We're here. And there's the cinema. And there's the supermarket. The shopping centre is next to the supermarket. See?
  **Woman 2** Could you 4_____, please? More slowly.

3 **Kate** There's 5_____, so there's no water in the kitchen or the bathroom. But there's water under the receptionist's desk! Poor Marina.
  **Simon** Sorry, did you say there's a problem on the street? 6_____, a problem with the water?

🔧 **Skill** checking information

If you don't understand what someone says, you can:
• ask him/her to repeat: *Could you repeat that, please?*   *Could you say that again?*
• ask him/her to speak more slowly: *Could you speak more slowly, please?*
• ask a question to check the information: *Did you say near the supermarket?*   *You mean, a problem with the water?*

**7 A** ▶ 6.16 Read the Skill box. Listen and match phrases a–d with conversations 1–4. Where are the people in the situations?

a Sorry, did you say …?   ____
b Sorry, could you say that again, please?   ____
c Sorry, could you repeat that, please?   ____
d Sorry, could you speak more slowly, please?   ____

**B** ▶ 6.16 Listen again and complete the information that the people repeat.

1 Turn right at the _____ .
  Then turn _____ at the _____ .
2 _____ . _____ @mail.com
3 70832 _____
4 £ _____

**Go to Communication practice:** Student A page 139, Student B page 147

**8 A** PREPARE In pairs, think of four places in your town. Think about how to get to the places from where you are now.

a train station or bus stop   a museum or tourist attraction
a restaurant or café   a shopping centre or supermarket

**B** PRACTISE Ask for and give directions. Check the information if you don't understand anything.

**C** PERSONAL BEST Swap partners and ask for and give directions to a new place. Are you more confident asking for directions in English?

**Personal Best** Write an email to a friend with directions to your house from the bus or train station.

# 5 and 6 REVIEW and PRACTICE

## Grammar

**1** Choose the correct options to complete the sentences.

1 On Saturday, I meet my friends _____ the shopping centre.
   a on     b under     c in

2 _____ any shelves in the living room.
   a There aren't
   b There are
   c There isn't

3 He can't _____ cakes. They're always horrible!
   a make     b to make     c makes

4 My friends live in the city. I meet _____ at the weekend.
   a they     b them     c us

5 There are _____ in the kitchen.
   a any biscuits
   b some biscuit
   c some biscuits

6 Your sunglasses are _____ to my laptop.
   a on     b in front     c next

7 A Is there a hospital in your town?
   B Yes, _____ .
   a there's
   b there is
   c there are

8 _____ drive a lorry?
   a Do you can
   b Can you
   c You can

**2** Complete the conversations with the words in the box.

| aren't | any | can | can't | her |
| isn't | it | next to | on | them |

1 A _____ you swim?
   B Yes, I can, but there _____ a swimming pool in this town.

2 A Are there _____ restaurants near here?
   B Yes, there's an Italian restaurant _____ the supermarket on School Road.

3 A Where are my headphones? I want to use _____ .
   B They're _____ the desk.

4 A Who can speak Spanish? I _____ read this menu.
   B Give _____ to me. I know some Spanish.

5 A Selina's class is at 8.00 p.m., but there _____ any buses in the evening.
   B It's OK. I can drive _____ to the class.

**3** Choose the correct options to complete the text.

### A treehouse with a difference

If you want an unusual house, Jono Williams can ¹ *make / makes* one for you. He's an engineer and he loves treehouses, but his new Skysphere is different – it's very small and it isn't ² *in / under* a tree!

**What's in the Skysphere?**
³ *There's / There are* a large bed, a TV and ⁴ *any / some* shelves. There's even a fridge for drinks ⁵ *between / in* the sofa! The windows are very large and Jono ⁶ *can / can't* see 360° around the house. There's Wi-Fi and he can ⁷ *use / using* his smartphone to play music and change the lights.

**What does Jono do there?**
Jono meets his friends at the Skysphere. They love ⁸ *them / it* too. They like listening to music and at night they can watch the stars.

**Are there ⁹ *some / any* problems with Jono's house?**
Only one … there ¹⁰ *isn't / aren't* a bathroom or a toilet.

## Vocabulary

**1** Put the words in the box in the correct columns.

| museum | lamp | table | DVD player | remote control |
| head | teeth | park | chair | Sat Nav | laptop | desk |
| police station | post office | face | foot |

| Places in a town | Electronic devices | Parts of the body | Furniture |
| --- | --- | --- | --- |
|  |  |  |  |

58

**REVIEW and PRACTICE  5 and 6**

**2** Circle the word that is different. Explain your answers.
1  toilet      bath         table        shower
2  ear         mouth        nose         hand
3  school      supermarket  restaurant   café
4  bank        kitchen      bedroom      living room
5  chair       arm          fridge       wardrobe
6  walking     reading      swimming     cycling
7  sing        speak        travel       call
8  DVD player  shelves      computer     Sat Nav

**3** Choose the correct options to complete the sentences.
1  My city has two _____ .
   a  wardrobes    b  hospitals    c  bathrooms
2  What time does the bus _____ in the city centre?
   a  arrive       b  travel       c  go out
3  Her _____ is long and brown.
   a  eye          b  hair         c  mouth
4  There's a large _____ in the living room.
   a  bath         b  leg          c  sofa
5  She always uses _____ to listen to music on the bus.
   a  earphones    b  TV           c  shelves
6  A  Where's the _____ ?   B  It's in the car.
   a  museum       b  toilet       c  Sat Nav
7  Is there any cheese in the _____ ?
   a  shower       b  fridge       c  DVR
8  At the weekend, I like _____ at the cinema.
   a  dancing      b  sleeping     c  watching films

**4** Complete the conversations with the words in the boxes.

bedroom  cooker  windows  desk  nightclub  cooking

**Ama**  Hi, Ed! How are you? Do you like your new flat?
**Ed**   No, not really. It's above a noisy ¹_____ .
**Ama**  Oh no! Is it big?
**Ed**   No, it's very small. In the ²_____ , there's only a bed and a ³_____ , and there aren't any ⁴_____ in the bathroom.
**Ama**  How's the kitchen? I know you like ⁵_____ .
**Ed**   It's dirty and the ⁶_____ is very old … but it's a good flat.
**Ama**  What's good about it?
**Ed**   It's cheap!

call  station  office  speak  drive  stop

**Sam**  Excuse me. Do you ⁷_____ English?
**Fran** Yes, I do.
**Sam**  Where's the bus ⁸_____ ?
**Fran** It's in front of the post ⁹_____ , but there aren't any buses today.
**Sam**  OK. Is there a train ¹⁰_____ near here?
**Fran** Yes, but it's a long walk. I can ¹¹_____ you there if you want.
**Sam**  No thanks, I can ¹²_____ a taxi.

# Personal Best

**Lesson 5A**  Write one positive and one negative sentence about your abilities.

**Lesson 6A**  Name five places in your town.

**Lesson 5B**  Name four electronic devices that you use.

**Lesson 6A**  Write three questions to find out what there is in a friend's town.

**Lesson 5C**  Name two activities that you like doing and two activities that you don't like doing.

**Lesson 6B**  Write your opinion of a famous building.

**Lesson 5C**  Write four sentences with different object pronouns.

**Lesson 6B**  Name five parts of the body that you have two of.

**Lesson 5D**  Write four sentences to describe yourself.

**Lesson 6C**  Name four things in your house and describe where they are.

**Lesson 5D**  Say why you like/don't like your town/city using *because*.

**Lesson 6D**  Write directions from the classroom to a shop, café, school or bus stop.

59

# UNIT 7 All in the past

**LANGUAGE** past simple: *be* ■ celebrities

## 7A When they were young

1 Match the jobs in the box with pictures a–f.

musician   politician   film director   writer   footballer   fashion model

Go to Vocabulary practice: celebrities, page 123

2 In pairs, describe celebrities. Can your partner guess who it is?

A *She's a tennis player. She's American. She's very good!*   B *Is it Serena Williams?*

3 A Read the introduction of the text. Match the blue sign with one of the people a–e.

B Read the rest of the text. Match the other people with descriptions 1–4 and write their names on the blue signs. Check their names on page 139.

Sir ALFRED HITCHCOCK 1899–1980 Film Director lived here 1926–1939

# London's famous houses

London was home to lots of famous people from all over the world. Who were they and where were their houses? It's easy – just look for the blue signs on the buildings!

**1869–1948 Lived here as a law student**

**1** He was a famous Indian politician, but he was also a student in London for three years. He was a vegetarian and in the 19th century it wasn't easy to find good vegetarian food in the city.

**1945–1981 Singer and musician Lived here 1972**

**2** In 1972, London was home to this Jamaican singer and his band. The musicians weren't famous then, but a year later their song *Stir It Up* was a big hit.

**1890–1976 Writer Lived here 1934–1941**

**3** This British writer wasn't from London, but she was here for seven years. Her crime stories were very popular around the world, and you probably know her famous detective – Hercule Poirot.

**1853–1890 Artist Lived here 1873–1874**

**4** This was the Dutch artist's home when he was 19 years old. He was in love with the owner's daughter, Eugenie. But was she interested in him? No, she wasn't!

60

past simple: *be* ■ celebrities   **LANGUAGE**   **7A**

**4  A** Complete the sentences with the words in the box. Check your answers in the text.

> was (x2)   were (x2)   wasn't   weren't

1  Where _____ their houses?
2  He _____ a famous Indian politician.
3  It _____ easy to find good vegetarian food.
4  The musicians _____ famous then.
5  Her crime stories _____ very popular.
6  _____ she interested in him?

**B** Complete the rules. Then read the Grammar box.
1  The past simple forms of *is/isn't* = _____ / _____ .
2  The past simple forms of *are/aren't* = _____ / _____ .

### Grammar   past simple: *be*

**Positive:**
He **was** a musician.
They **were** singers.

**Negative:**
I **wasn't** an actor.
You **weren't** famous.

**Questions:**
**Was** she a writer?
**Were** you happy?

**Short answers:**
Yes, she **was**.   No, she **wasn't**.
Yes, we **were**.   No, we **weren't**.

Go to Grammar practice: past simple: *be*, page 102

**5  A**  ▶ 7.3  **Pronunciation:** *was/were* Listen and repeat the question and answer. How are *was* and *were* pronounced?

A  *Where were you yesterday?*
B  *I was at work.*

**B** In pairs, ask and answer the question *Where were you …?* with the times in the boxes. Pay attention to the pronunciation of *was* and *were*.

A  *Where were you at 7.30 this morning?*  B  *I was on the bus. I always go to work early. What about you?*
A  *I was in bed!*

> at 7.30 this morning    yesterday morning    yesterday at 2.00 p.m.    yesterday evening

Go to Communication practice: Student A page 139, Student B page 147

**6** ▶ 7.4  Complete the sentences with the correct form of *was* or *were*. Listen and check.

# When they were young

- Singer Justin Timberlake and actor Ryan Gosling ¹_____ presenters on a children's TV show when they ²_____ young.

- In 1990, J.K. Rowling ³_____ an English teacher in Portugal, but she ⁴_____ happy there. Seven years later, she ⁵_____ famous all over the world as the writer of the *Harry Potter* books.

- Actors and film directors Matt Damon and Ben Affleck ⁶_____ at school together, but they ⁷_____ in the same class.

- Athlete Usain Bolt ⁸_____ interested in cricket and football at school. His teachers ⁹_____ surprised because he ¹⁰_____ a very, very fast runner!

**7** In pairs, ask and answer questions about when you were young. Use the ideas below.

A  *What was the name of your first teacher?*  B  *Mrs Fuentes. She was really nice. What about you?*

1  What / the name of your first teacher?
2  / you a good student?
3  / you in a big class?
4  Who / your best friend?
5  What celebrities / popular when you / a child?
6  What films / popular?
7  What / your favourite TV programmes?
8  What / your favourite food?

**Personal Best**  Think of someone famous that you like. Write a paragraph about their life when they were young.

61

# 7 SKILLS LISTENING    listening for dates ■ linking consonants and vowels ■ months and ordinals

## 7B I was there in July

**1** Order the months from 1–12.

- ☐ April
- ☐ August
- ☐ December
- ☐ February
- [1] January
- ☐ July
- ☐ June
- ☐ March
- ☐ May
- ☐ November
- ☐ October
- ☐ September

**May**

| 1 a | 2 | 3 b | 4 | 5 | 6 | 7 |
|---|---|---|---|---|---|---|
| 8 | 9 | 10 | 11 | 12 | 13 c | 14 |
| 15 | 16 | 17 | 18 | 19 | 20 d | 21 |
| 22 | 23 | 24 | 25 | 26 | 27 | 28 e |
| 29 | 30 | 31 f | | | | |

**2** Look at the calendar. Match days a–f with dates 1–6.

1 the thirty-first of May ____
2 the twentieth of May ____
3 the twenty-eighth of May ____
4 the twelfth of May ____
5 the first of May ____
6 the third of May ____

Go to Vocabulary practice: months and ordinals, page 124

**3** Ask and answer the questions in pairs.

1 What's the date today?
2 When's your birthday?
3 What's your favourite month?
4 When was the last public holiday?

**4 A** Look at the picture. What do you know about Shakespeare?

**B** Complete the text with the words in the box.

April   Hamlet   plays   writer

William Shakespeare was a famous British [1]_____. He was born on 26 [2]_____ 1564 and he died in April 1616. His [3]_____ are popular all over the world. They include *Romeo and Juliet*, [4]_____ and *Othello*.

**5** ▶ 7.7  Watch or listen to the first part of *Learning Curve*. Are the sentences true (T) or false (F)?

1 Shakespeare's plays are only about British people. ____
2 The Globe Theatre was Shakespeare's first theatre. ____
3 'Shakespeare in the Park' in New York is very expensive. ____
4 You can read Shakespeare's plays in 80 different languages. ____

### Skill   listening for dates

It's sometimes important to listen for specific years and months.

- Listen carefully because some months sound similar: *September, November* and *December*.
- Years are usually divided into two numbers: *1990 = nineteen ninety, 2008 = twenty oh eight*. For years after 2000, we sometimes use the whole number: *2009 = two thousand and nine*.
- We use ordinals to talk about centuries (100 years): *1900–1999 = the twentieth century*.

**6** ▶ 7.7  Read the Skill box. Watch or listen again. Complete the texts with the correct information.

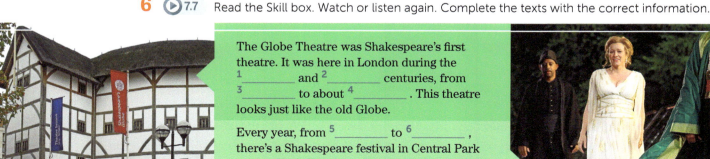

The Globe Theatre was Shakespeare's first theatre. It was here in London during the [1]_____ and [2]_____ centuries, from [3]_____ to about [4]_____. This theatre looks just like the old Globe.

Every year, from [5]_____ to [6]_____, there's a Shakespeare festival in Central Park in New York City. It's called 'Shakespeare in the Park'. 1,800 people can see a Shakespeare play at the Delacorte Theater for free!

listening for dates ■ linking consonants and vowels ■ months and ordinals  **LISTENING**  **SKILLS**  **7B**

**7** ▶ 7.8  Watch or listen to the rest of the show. Match the people with sentences 1–4.

1 This person likes plays about love. _____
2 This person works at a theatre. _____
3 This person doesn't like Shakespeare. _____
4 This person likes plays about history. _____

**8** ▶ 7.8  Watch or listen again. Answer the questions with months or years.
1 When does Marty come to New York?  _____ and _____
2 When were Elizabeth and Henry in Cambridge?  _____
3 When was *A Midsummer Night's Dream* in Beijing?  _____
4 When was *Henry IV* at the Hong Kong Arts Festival?  _____

**9** Ask and answer the questions in pairs.

> Do you ever go to the theatre?
> Which Shakespeare plays do you know?
> Which types of plays do you like?
> Do you like Shakespeare? Why/Why not?

**10** ▶ 7.9  Listen to Penny's sentence and look at the linked words. Pay attention to how the sounds join together.

> A lot‿of people‿are here‿in the queue for theatre tickets.

 **Listening builder**  linking consonants and vowels

When a word ends in a consonant sound, and the next word starts with a vowel sound, we usually link the sounds together.
*Hamlet‿is about‿a prince‿in Denmark.*
*I'm‿Elizabeth‿and this‿is my husband, Henry.*
*Sometimes the plays‿are‿in‿English‿and Chinese.*

**11** ▶ 7.10  Read the Listening builder. Then listen and complete the sentences.
1 Hi, my name's Lucas _____ _____ _____ _____ .
2 In _____ _____ _____ _____ New York City for the first time.
3 The play _____ _____ _____ _____ king.
4 She was born on the _____ _____ _____ , 1999.
5 I like *Hamlet*, but I _____ _____ _____ the story.

**12** Look at the pictures. Discuss the questions in pairs.

1 When was the last time you were at a theatre/a cinema/a concert?
2 Which play/film/band was it?
3 Was it good? Why/Why not?

  Write a description of your favourite play or film. Where does it happen? What's it about?

# 7 LANGUAGE   past simple: regular verbs ■ time expressions

## 7C Famous decades

**1** Match the decades in the box with a–f.

> the nineties   the twenty-tens   the seventies   the noughties   the sixties   the eighties

a
b
c
d
e
f

**2** Discuss the questions in pairs.

*I was born in the eighties. What about you?*

1 In which decade were you born?
2 Which decade has the best music and fashion, in your opinion?
3 Which was your favourite decade? Why?

**3** ▶ 7.11   In pairs, complete the quiz with the years in the box. Listen and check.

> 1969   1973   1985   1991   2004   2012

## The Decades Quiz

On 4 February ¹_____ , Mark Zuckerberg started Facebook from his bedroom at university. He wanted 500 people to join. Now, more than 1.5 billion people use it!

In ⁴_____ , Korean singer Psy danced *Gangnam Style* all over the world. The song was number 1 in 37 countries. Did you watch the video?

 On 20 July ²_____ , Neil Armstrong and Buzz Aldrin walked on the moon. 600 million people watched on TV or listened on the radio.

 On 30 November ⁵_____ , the USA and Norway played in the first Women's Football World Cup final in China. The result was a 2–1 win for the USA.

In April ³_____ , Coca-Cola® tried a new recipe for their drink. People didn't like the flavour, and three months later, the original Coca-Cola was back in the shops.

On 3 April ⁶_____ , Martin Cooper from Motorola called Joel Engel on the world's first mobile phone. Joel quickly stopped the call because he wasn't happy. He worked for rival company AT&T!

**4** Read the quiz again. Write the past simple form of verbs 1–8.

1 start _____   3 watch _____   5 dance _____   7 call _____
2 walk _____   4 try _____   6 play _____   8 stop _____

**5 A** Look at the verbs in exercise 4 again and complete the rules.

1 We usually add the letters ____ to verbs to make the past simple form.
2 If the verb ends in -e, we add the letter ____ to make the past simple form.
3 If the verb ends in consonant + y, we remove the y and add the letters ____ to make the past simple form.
4 If the verb ends in consonant + vowel + consonant, we double the last consonant and add ____.

**B** Complete the sentences from the text to make the negative and question forms of the past simple. Does the main verb change form? Read the Grammar box.

1 People _____ like the flavour.   2 _____ you watch the video?

past simple: regular verbs ■ time expressions    LANGUAGE  **7C**

### Grammar — past simple: regular verbs

**Positive:**
600 million people **watched** on TV.
Coca-Cola **tried** a new recipe.

**Negative:**
They **didn't call** on a smartphone.
Brazil **didn't play** in the final.

**Questions and short answers:**
**Did** you **try** the new drink?
Yes, I **did**.   No, I **didn't**.

Go to Grammar practice: past simple: regular verbs, page 102

**6** ▶ 7.13  Complete the text with the past simple form of the verbs in brackets. Listen and check.

### Were the nineties the best decade for films?

My brother [1]_____ (study) films at university and he thinks the nineties were the best decade for cinema. So last week, I [2]_____ (decide) to watch the film *Titanic* for the first time. It was in the cinema 20 years ago, but I was only two then.
I [3]_____ (love) it … but it's a sad story. It's about a real disaster that [4]_____ (happen) in 1912 in the Atlantic Ocean. Thousands of people [5]_____ (die) because the ship [6]_____ (not carry) enough lifeboats.
After that, I [7]_____ (want) to see more films from the nineties. So at the weekend, I [8]_____ (watch) *Jurassic Park*, *Forrest Gump* and *Pulp Fiction*. On Monday, it was *Toy Story*, and last night, I [9]_____ (start) watching *The Matrix* … but I [10]_____ (not finish) it because at 1.00 a.m. I [11]_____ (need) to go to bed. My brother was right – films from the nineties are amazing!

**7** Complete the time expressions with the words in the box. Check your answers in the text in exercise 6.

in   ago   last (x2)   on   at (x2)

1  20 years _____      3  _____ 1912          5  _____ night        7  _____ 1.00 a.m.
2  _____ week          4  _____ the weekend   6  _____ Monday

Go to Vocabulary practice: time expressions, page 124

**8 A** ▶ 7.15  **Pronunciation:** -*ed* endings Listen and repeat the sentences from the text.
Pay attention to the -*ed* endings in **bold**: /d/, /t/ and /ɪd/.

1  /d/   lov**ed**      I lov**ed** it.
2  /t/   watch**ed**    I watch**ed** *Jurassic Park*.
3  /ɪd/  need**ed**     I need**ed** to go to bed.

**B** ▶ 7.16  Write the verbs in the box in the correct columns. Listen, check and repeat.

danced   wanted   played   tried   walked   visited

| /d/ | /t/ | /ɪd/ |
|---|---|---|
|   |   |   |

Go to Communication practice: Student A page 139, Student B page 147

**9 A** In pairs, ask and answer the questions with the past simple form of the verbs. Write your partner's answers in the table.

**A** *When did you last watch a film on DVD?*   **B** *I watched a film on DVD about a year ago.*

| When did you last … | Answers |
|---|---|
| 1  watch / a film on DVD? |  |
| 2  study / for an exam? |  |
| 3  cook / chicken? |  |
| 4  play / a musical instrument? |  |
| 5  call / a friend on the phone? |  |

| When was the last time you … | Answers |
|---|---|
| 6  use / a computer? |  |
| 7  dance / with friends? |  |
| 8  relax / at home? |  |
| 9  talk / to a neighbour? |  |
| 10  listen / to the radio? |  |

**B** Tell the class about your partner.
*Marco watched a film on DVD about a year ago.*

**Personal Best**  Choose six different time expressions and write a true past simple sentence for each one.

65

# 7 SKILLS  WRITING  writing informal emails ■ sequencers

## 7D A weekend away

**1** In pairs, order the pictures from 1–6 to make a story about Elena and her father's trip to Oxford.

**2** Read Elena's email and check the order of the pictures in exercise 1.

---

**To:** Becky Stewart
**Subject:** My weekend

Hi Becky,

How are things? I hope you're well.

Did I tell you about last weekend? I visited my sister Hannah. She lives in Oxford now. I wanted to go on my own … but Dad decided to come with me!

We travelled by train on Saturday. We arrived in Oxford and Hannah was at the train station. In the afternoon, we explored the city. First, we walked round the university. It was beautiful, but Dad stopped to take hundreds of photos! Then we visited an art gallery. Dad studied every painting and looked at every sculpture – we were there for hours! After that, Hannah and I wanted to go shopping, but Dad wanted to visit a museum. It was so boring!

It was a disaster! This weekend, I want to stay at home, or go away without Dad!
See you soon.
Elena

---

**3 A** Read the email again. Are the sentences true (T) or false (F)?

1 Elena and her dad travelled to Oxford. ____
2 They stayed in Oxford for a week. ____
3 Elena's dad didn't like the university. ____
4 They explored the university on foot. ____
5 They didn't stay in the art gallery for a long time. ____
6 Hannah and Elena didn't want to visit the museum. ____

**B** Look at the email again and answer the questions. Then read the Skill box.

1 How does Elena start her email?
2 How does she ask how her friend is?
3 How does she introduce her news?
4 How does she finish her email?

### 🔧 Skill  writing informal emails

We write informal emails to friends and people we know well.
- Start the email in a friendly way: *Hi …, Hello …*
- Ask about the person: *How are you? How are things? I hope you're well.*
- Say why you are writing: *Did I tell you about …? I wanted to tell/ask you …*
- Finish the email in a friendly way: *See you soon, Bye for now, Take care.*

writing informal emails ■ sequencers  **WRITING**  **SKILLS**  **7D**

**4** Complete the email with the words in the box.

hope   how   hello   tell   now

**To:** George Hawkins
**Subject:** Fantastic weekend

¹_____ George,
²_____ are you? I ³_____ you and the family are well.
I wanted to ⁴_____ you about last weekend. My daughter Elena and I travelled to Oxford. My other daughter, Hannah, moved there a few months ago, so we stayed with her.
On Saturday, we walked into town. First, we explored the university. It was very interesting. Elena loved all the old buildings! Then we visited an art gallery. We were there for hours – the girls didn't want to leave! After that, we looked around the museum. I was quite tired, but the girls really enjoyed it. It was a great weekend. I think Elena wants to do it again soon.
Bye for ⁵_____ .
Frank

**5** Discuss the questions in pairs.
1 Who is Frank?
2 What differences are there between Frank and Elena's emails?
3 Do you enjoy visiting art galleries and museums? Why/Why not?

**6** Order sentences a–c from 1–3. Check your answers in the email in exercise 4.
a ☐ After that, we looked around the museum.
b ☐ First, we explored the university.
c ☐ Then we visited an art gallery.

**Text builder    sequencers**

We can show the order of events with *First*, *Then* and *After that*:
*First*, we walked into town.   *Then* we visited the university.   *After that*, we explored the centre.
**Look!** We usually use a comma after *First* and *After that*.

**7** Read the Text builder. Then write sentences in the past simple with sequencers.
*First, we listened to some music. Then we cooked dinner ...*
1 We / listen to / some music. We / cook / dinner. We / watch / a film.
2 She / visit / her sister. She / call / her mum. She / talk to / her dad.
3 I / walk to / my friend's house. We / study / English together. We / play / football.

**8 A PREPARE** Think of a weekend when you were somewhere interesting.
Make notes about what happened. Think about:
• where you travelled to      • where you stayed
• how you travelled            • the places that you visited
• who was with you             • if you enjoyed it

Use these regular verbs to help you:

visit   travel   play   walk   watch   listen to   wait   love
cook   explore   stay   talk   enjoy   need   want   try

**B PRACTISE** Write an email to a friend about your weekend.
Use the Skill box and Text builder to help you.

**C PERSONAL BEST** Swap your email with your partner. Does your partner use the past simple correctly? Can you correct any mistakes?

**Personal Best**  Write about a day when you visited a lot of places, like Elena's day in Oxford.

67

# UNIT 8 Travel

**LANGUAGE** past simple: irregular verbs ■ travel verbs

## 8A Incredible journeys

1 Complete the sentences with the verbs in the box.

get lost   book   fly   miss   ride   take

1 Some of my friends _____ motorbikes to work.

3 I sometimes _____ the bus because I get up late.

5 I never _____ because I don't like it!

2 I always _____ train tickets early to get a good price.

4 If I go out at night, I usually _____ a taxi home.

6 I often _____ in a new town.

Go to Vocabulary practice: travel verbs, page 125

2 In pairs, say the sentences in exercise 1. Decide if they are true or false for your partner.

A *Some of my friends ride motorbikes to work.*   B *False.*
A *You're right. All my friends drive to work.*

3 Look at the title and the picture. In pairs, guess what the story is about. Read the text and check.

## Around the world *for love*

In January 2001, Ian Johnstone from Yorkshire in the UK went to work in Australia for a year, but his girlfriend Amy stayed at home. It was difficult to be so far away from her and after six months, Ian planned to visit her. He wanted to ask her to marry him, but he didn't tell her about his plans … it was a surprise visit!

Ian booked a flight and in July he flew from Sydney to London, with a stop in Singapore. But he didn't know about Amy's plans. She also wanted to surprise Ian with a visit, and at that exact moment, she was also on a plane … to Australia!

When Ian arrived in London, he bought some flowers and took the train to Yorkshire. Amy wasn't at home, so Ian waited for her. At the same time, Amy arrived at Ian's flat in Sydney. When his flatmate told her that Ian was 17,000 km away in England, Amy thought that it was a joke!

It wasn't possible for Ian or Amy to change their tickets, so they didn't see each other. But the story had a happy ending. Ian called Amy and asked her to marry him. And what did she say? She said 'yes', of course!

past simple: irregular verbs ■ travel verbs    **LANGUAGE**    **8A**

**4** Are the sentences true (T) or false (F)? Read the text again and check.
1 Ian went to Australia with Amy. ____
2 He wanted to see his girlfriend. ____
3 Amy lived in London. ____
4 She travelled to Australia to see Ian. ____
5 They changed their tickets. ____
6 Amy didn't want to marry Ian. ____

**5 A** Look at the past simple verbs in **bold** in the sentence from the text. Which verb is regular and which is irregular?

Ian **booked** a flight and in July he **flew** from Sydney to London.

**B** Find the past simple form of the irregular verbs in the text. Then read the Grammar box.
1 go _____  2 fly _flew_  3 buy _____  4 take _____  5 think _____  6 say _____

### Grammar — past simple: irregular verbs

Positive:
Ian **went** to work in Australia.
He **flew** to London.
He **bought** some flowers.

Negative:
Ian **didn't go** to work in Singapore.
He **didn't fly** to Sydney.
He **didn't buy** chocolate.

Questions:
**Did** Ian **go** home?
**Did** he **fly** alone?
**Did** he **buy** a ring?

Short answers:
Yes, he **did**.
No, he **didn't**.

Go to Grammar practice: past simple: irregular verbs, page 103

**6** Complete the text with the past simple form of the verbs in brackets.

## Around the world – on foot!
This is Jean Béliveau, a Canadian who walked around the world, through 64 countries in 11 years!

When ¹_____ he _____ (leave)?
Jean ²_____ (leave) his home on 18 August 2000, and he ³_____ (not get) home until 2011.
His wife, Luce, ⁴_____ (not go) with him, but she ⁵_____ (fly) to meet him eleven times.
Where ⁶_____ he _____ (sleep)?
He ⁷_____ (sleep) in people's homes, parks, schools, hospitals – and even in a police station!
People also ⁸_____ (buy) him food and drink.
Why ⁹_____ he _____ (do) it?
He ¹⁰_____ (do) it because he wanted people to know about children's lives in other countries.

**7 A** ▶8.3 **Pronunciation:** irregular past simple verbs Listen and repeat the past simple verbs. Pay attention to the vowel sounds /ɒ/, /ɔː/ and /əʊ/.
1 /ɒ/  got  lost   2 /ɔː/  bought  thought   3 /əʊ/  rode  drove

**B** ▶8.4 Underline the words in the sentences with the same vowel sounds. Listen, check and repeat.
1 I got on the bus.
2 We all bought a ticket.
3 I rode home on my bike.
4 He lost his new watch.
5 I thought it was a horse.
6 She drove to my home.

Go to Communication practice: Student A page 140, Student B page 148

**8 A** ▶8.5 Read Leanne's plans for a holiday to Croatia last summer. Then listen and correct the information with what really happened.

**B** In pairs, make sentences about Leanne's trip.
*She didn't fly from Manchester. She flew from London.*

### My trip to Croatia
24 July: fly from Manchester to Dubrovnik
30 July: take bus to Split
5 August: sail to Šolta
10 August: take train to Zagreb and fly home
**Activities:** eat local food, swim in the sea, take photos ... fall in love?

**9** Think about a holiday or journey. In pairs, ask and answer the questions in the boxes.

Where did you go?   How did you travel?   What did you do?
When did you go?   Who did you go with?   Did you have a good time?

**Personal Best**  Write about your partner's holiday or journey from exercise 9.

69

# 8 SKILLS READING understanding the main idea ■ modifiers ■ weather and seasons

## 8B Crazy weather!

**1** Match the weather phrases in the box with pictures a–d on page 71.

> It's cold.   It's sunny.   It's raining.   It's windy.

**Go to Vocabulary practice:** weather and seasons, page 126

**2** In pairs, talk about the seasons in your country. Use *love/like/don't like/hate*.
*I don't like autumn because it rains and it's cold and windy.*

### Skill   understanding the main idea

When you see a text for the first time, try to understand the main idea quickly.
- Look at the title and pictures.
- Read the first line of each paragraph.
- Use this information to understand what the text is about.

**3 A** Read the Skill box. Then read the title and the highlighted sentences on page 71. Tick (✓) the main idea.
- a Robbie had lots of problems with transport in Germany.  ☐
- b Robbie went on holiday and the weather changed a lot.  ☐
- c Robbie was in Berlin in the summer, but it snowed all week.  ☐
- d Robbie didn't like the weather in Germany, so he went to Ireland.  ☐

**B** Read the whole text and check.

**4** Are the sentences true (T) or false (F)? Read the text again and check.
1 Robbie went to Berlin with his girlfriend.  ____
2 They had ice cream in Viktoria Park.  ____
3 They waited on a train for three hours.  ____
4 It rained at the Television Tower.  ____
5 They didn't go to the concert because it snowed.  ____
6 They arrived at the airport late and missed the flight.  ____

**5** Match the halves to make sentences from the text. Do the modifiers in **bold** come before or after the adjectives?
1 When we got off the plane, it was **very**
2 When we got to the park, it was **quite**
3 And in the afternoon, it was **really**
4 The views were**n't very**

a cold.
b good.
c windy.
d hot and sunny.

### Text builder   modifiers

We use modifiers before an adjective to make the meaning stronger or less strong:

▼ **really/very**    It was **really** sunny. The film was **very** exciting.
  **quite**        The museum was **quite** interesting.
  **not very**     The food was**n't very** good.

**6** Read the Text builder. Then write sentences with the words and a modifier.
*The weather today is very hot.*
1 the weather today / hot
2 the *Star Wars* films / exciting
3 I think English / difficult
4 public transport in my country / expensive
5 my street / noisy
6 people in my city / friendly

**7** In pairs, talk about your last trip or holiday. What was the weather like?
*Last year, I visited Morocco. It was very hot and sunny in the day, and really cold at night.*

understanding the main idea ■ modifiers ■ weather and seasons    **READING**    SKILLS  **8B**

# Travel news

## Four Seasons In One Week

Robbie Irwin

### Monday 12 March

My girlfriend and I arrived in Berlin today on holiday. We thought Germany was cold in March, so we only brought winter clothes, but we had a surprise. When we got off the plane, it was very hot and sunny! So this afternoon, we went to the shops and bought shorts and T-shirts and walked around the city centre. I even had an ice cream!

### Wednesday 14 March

Today we decided to visit Viktoria Park, but the weather changed. It was warm when we left the hotel, so we wore our new shorts and T-shirts. But when we got to the park, it was quite cold. And in the afternoon, it was really windy. We decided to visit Museum Island, so we took a train back into the city … but a tree fell on the tracks, and we didn't move for three hours! After that, we went back to the hotel, changed our clothes and had dinner in a restaurant.

### Thursday 15 March

The weather here is crazy – this morning it was sunny again! We decided to visit the famous Television Tower. It's over 350m tall and I wanted to take some photos of the city. But when we got to the top of the tower, it was cloudy and it started to rain – the views weren't very good. We bought some umbrellas and went to see a concert. When we came out – guess what? It was warm and sunny again!

### Saturday 17 March

I can't believe it – it's 11.00 p.m. and we're still in Berlin Airport! It's really cold and it snowed all day. We took a taxi to the airport and when we arrived, we saw that there were no flights. The next flight is tomorrow morning at 7.00 a.m.

### Sunday 18 March

Finally, we're back home in Ireland. We had bad luck with the weather, but we had a great trip and we loved Berlin.

a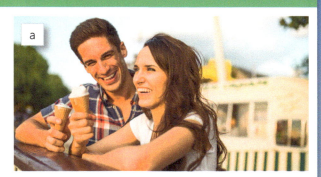

b

c

d

**Personal Best**  Write a paragraph about the weather in your town or city in different seasons.

# 8 LANGUAGE  *there was/were* ■ nature

## 8C Then and now

**1** Match the words in the box with the parts of the picture 1–6.

| sky | field | forest | mountain | river | tree |

1 _____   4 _____
2 _____   5 _____
3 _____   6 _____

**Go to Vocabulary practice:** nature, page 127

**2** Discuss the questions in pairs.

1 Which country is the picture in exercise 1?
2 What nature can you see out of the window?
3 Do you prefer beaches, mountains or forests? Why?

**3** Read the introduction to a radio show. Answer the questions.

1 How many people live in Shenzhen? _____
2 Where does Liu Jiang live now? _____
3 What's her job? _____
4 When was she last in Shenzhen? _____

## Then and Now: Shenzhen, China

In the 1970s, Shenzhen was a small fishing town. Today, it is an enormous city of 12 million people. Liu Jiang, a Chinese-American writer from Chicago, lived in Shenzhen as a child. Listen as she returns to the city for the first time in 30 years.

**Sunday 28 June, 9.00 p.m.**  Radio 7

**4** ▶ 8.8 Listen to the radio show. Tick (✓) the things that Shenzhen had 30 years ago and has today.

|  | Fields | Forest | Tall buildings | River | Train station | Airport | University |
|---|---|---|---|---|---|---|---|
| Shenzhen 30 years ago |  |  |  |  |  |  |  |
| Shenzhen today |  |  |  |  |  |  |  |

**5 A** ▶ 8.8 Match the halves to make sentences and questions. Listen again and check.

1 **There were** fields         a or buses?
2 **There was** a forest        b here before.
3 **There weren't** any cars    c – everyone had bicycles.
4 **Was there** public transport d to travel around the country?
5 **Were there** any trains     e where we played.
6 **There wasn't** a university f around the town.

**B** Look at the words in **bold** in sentences 1–6 again. Choose the correct options to complete the rules. Then read the Grammar box.

1 We use *there was* and *there were* to talk about *the present / the past*.
2 We use *there was* and *there wasn't* with *singular / plural* nouns.
3 We use *there were* and *there weren't* with *singular / plural* nouns.

there was/were ■ nature    LANGUAGE  8C

### Grammar  there was/were

| Positive: | Negative: | Questions | Short answers: |
|---|---|---|---|
| **There was** a train station. | **There wasn't** an airport. | **Was there** a university? | Yes, **there was**.  No, **there wasn't**. |
| **There were** lots of trees. | **There weren't** any cars. | **Were there** any shops? | Yes, **there were**.  No, **there weren't**. |

Go to Grammar practice: *there was/were*, page 103

**6** Complete the text with the correct forms of *there was/were*.

This is Pompeii in Italy. In AD 79, a volcano destroyed the city. But what was life like for the 20,000 people that lived there before? ¹_____ about 200 cafés in the town. They sold eggs, cheese, bread and fruit. ²_____ also a market.
Children did lessons outside or at home, so ³_____ any school buildings. ⁴_____ some doctors, but ⁵_____ a hospital.
⁶_____ a big amphitheatre, where ⁷_____ plays and concerts. And of course, ⁸_____ gladiators!

**7 A** ▶8.10  **Pronunciation:** sentence stress  Listen and repeat the questions and short answers. Pay attention to the underlined stressed words.

1 Was there a <u>train</u> <u>station</u>?    <u>Yes</u>, there <u>was</u>.
2 Was there an <u>airport</u>?    <u>No</u>, there <u>wasn't</u>.
3 Were there any <u>trees</u>?    <u>Yes</u>, there <u>were</u>.
4 Were there any <u>cars</u>?    <u>No</u>, there <u>weren't</u>.

**B** ▶8.11  In pairs, ask and answer questions 1–4 about Pompeii. Remember to stress the correct words. Listen, check and repeat.

1 Were there any cafés?
2 Was there a market?
3 Were there any school buildings?
4 Was there a hospital?

Go to Communication practice: Student A page 140, Student B page 148

**8** In pairs, look at the pictures and talk about Oxford Street in London in the past. Use the words in the box and your own ideas.

| buses   road   shops   horses and carriages   tall buildings   bus stops   street lights   taxis |

*There weren't any buses in the 19th century.*

Oxford Street, 19th century    Oxford Street, now

**9** How is your town or city different from the past? In pairs, talk about the differences.

*There was a cinema on Panama Street, but now there's a supermarket.*

**Personal Best**  Write about where you lived when you were a child.

73

# 8 SKILLS  SPEAKING  starting and ending a phone call at work ■ buying a ticket

## 8D  A trip to Canada

**1** Ask and answer the questions in pairs.

1 Why do you usually travel?
   a for work or study   b to visit friends or family   c to go on holiday   d other
2 How do you prefer to travel? Why?
   a to take the train   b to fly   c to drive   d other
3 How do you usually book your tickets when you travel?
   a online   b on the phone   c at a travel agent's   d other

**2 A** ▶ 8.12  Watch or listen to the first part of *Learning Curve*. Answer the questions.

1 Why does Marc want to travel?
2 How does he prefer to travel?
3 How does he book the tickets?

**B** ▶ 8.12  Are the sentences true (T) or false (F)? Watch or listen again and check.

1 Marc works with technology. ____
2 He never buys tickets online. ____
3 He loves flying. ____
4 Clarisse is Marc's friend. ____
5 It's hot and sunny in California. ____
6 The journey to Montreal is 11 hours. ____

**3** ▶ 8.13  Complete the questions with the words in the box. Listen and check.

> arrive   how   leave   when   return

1 **Clarisse** _____ do you want to leave?
  **Marc** March 11.
2 **Clarisse** When would you like to _____ ?
  **Marc** March 21.
3 **Marc** What time does the train _____ ?
  **Clarisse** The train leaves from New York at 8.15 a.m.
4 **Marc** And when does it _____ in Montreal?
  **Clarisse** 7.11 p.m.
5 **Marc** So, _____ much is it?
  **Clarisse** It's $138 for a return ticket.

### Conversation builder · buying a ticket

**Customer:**
*I'd like a single/return ticket to …*
*What time does the train/bus/flight leave?*
*What time/When does it arrive?*
*How much is it?*

**Assistant:**
*What kind of ticket would you like?*
*Would you like a single or return ticket?*
*When do you want to return/leave?*
*It's … for a single/return ticket.*

**4** Read the Conversation builder. Then in pairs, make conversations to buy the tickets.

A *I'd like a single ticket to Newcastle, please.*   B *When would you like to leave?*

Ticket type: SINGLE
Adults: ONE
From: LONDON KING'S CROSS
To: NEWCASTLE
Date: 14 JULY
Time: 12.05
Arrival: 14.55
Price: £65.00

OUTBOUND
Flight: RAX3498
Departing from: Frankfurt
21 September 10.00
Arriving at: Marrakesh
21 September 14.45

RETURN
Flight: RAX9912
Departing from: Marrakesh
5 October 12.35
Arriving at: Frankfurt
5 October 17.10

Price: €345.00

starting and ending a phone call at work ■ buying a ticket   SPEAKING   SKILLS  8D

**5 A** ▶ 8.14 Watch or listen to the second part of the show.
Do you think Marc enjoyed his trip? Why/Why not?

**B** ▶ 8.14 Choose the correct options to complete the sentences.
Watch or listen again to check.
1 Marc asks Clarisse about ____ .
   a  places to eat        b  places to stay      c  public transport
2 The Wi-Fi in Montreal isn't good when ____ .
   a  it snows             b  it rains            c  it's windy
3 On his trip, Marc helped people with their ____ .
   a  coffee and sandwiches  b  French            c  Wi-Fi

**6** ▶ 8.15 Listen to the phrases from the conversations. Are they for starting or ending a phone call?

1 Hello, *Bon Voyage Travel*. This is Clarisse.
2 Thanks. Goodbye.
3 Hello, my name is Marc Kim. I'm Penny's friend.
4 Thanks for calling.

🔧 **Skill**  starting and ending a phone call at work

When you speak on the telephone, remember to give important information and be polite.
• When you answer the phone, say *Hello* and identify yourself or your company: *Hello, Learning Curve. Hello, this is Clarisse / Clarisse speaking.*
• When you call someone, say who you are: *Hello, this is … , My name's …*
• When the conversation finishes, thank the person who called and say goodbye: *Thanks for calling. Thanks for your call.*

**7** ▶ 8.16 Complete the conversations with the missing words. Listen and check.

**Brad**   Hello, *Easy Travel*. Brad [1]_____ .
**Jenny**  Hi, [2]_____ is Jenny Foster. I'd like a single ticket to Seoul from Sydney, please.
…
**Brad**   OK, Jenny. You leave on 15 June at 08.15 and you arrive in Seoul at 17.05.
**Jenny**  Thanks very much.
**Brad**   You're welcome. Thanks for your [3]_____ .
**Jenny**  [4]_____ .

**Go to Communication practice:** Student A page 140, Student B page 148

**8 A** PREPARE  Choose a type of transport and write down the information.

train

bus

plane

ferry

• where you want to go
• what type of ticket you want
• when you want to leave
• if/when you want to return

**B** PRACTISE  Sit back-to-back with a partner. Act out a telephone call to buy a ticket. Then swap roles.

**C** PERSONAL BEST  Listen to another pair. Write down three things that they do well.

**Personal Best**  Write a conversation between a customer and a travel agent about a new trip.

# 7 and 8 REVIEW and PRACTICE

## Grammar

**1** Choose the correct options to complete the questions and sentences.

1 Where _____ last night?
  a you were
  b were you
  c you was

2 Our taxi driver _____ very friendly.
  a wasn't
  b not was
  c weren't

3 She _____ work at 7.00 p.m. last night.
  a did finish
  b finishes
  c finished

4 _____ football at the weekend?
  a Did you play
  b You did play
  c You played

5 They _____ to Oslo for a meeting.
  a did fly
  b flied
  c flew

6 We had a map, so we _____ lost.
  a didn't get
  b didn't got
  c not got

7 _____ a restaurant in your hotel?
  a There was
  b Was there
  c Were there

8 _____ two police officers in the street last night.
  a There was
  b They were
  c There were

**2** Rewrite the questions and sentences in the past simple.

1 Does she play tennis with Laura?
  _____ last weekend?

2 There are two eggs in the fridge.
  _____ last night.

3 I don't have time for breakfast.
  _____ this morning.

4 I ride my bike to work.
  _____ yesterday.

5 Do you go to the gym?
  _____ last Saturday?

6 He gets on the 8.00 a.m. train.
  _____ yesterday.

**3** Complete the text with the past simple form of the verbs in brackets.

### Birds for friends

In many countries people give food to birds in parks or in their gardens. But Gabi Mann from Seattle in the USA has a very special relationship with the birds in her neighbourhood – they bring *her* presents!
The story ¹_____ (start) when Gabi ²_____ (be) four years old. She ³_____ (have) some food in the car and when she ⁴_____ (get out), the food fell on the ground. There ⁵_____ (be) a crow near the car and it ⁶_____ (fly) down to eat the food. After that, Gabi ⁷_____ (not eat) all of her lunch at school. Instead she kept some and ⁸_____ (give) it to the birds on the way home. In 2013, she ⁹_____ (help) more birds and put food and water in the garden every morning. One day the crows started bringing things like buttons, rocks, small pieces of metal or plastic and even jewellery for Gabi. ¹⁰_____ they _____ (want) to say 'thank you' to her? Gabi thinks so. She collects these 'presents' and she now has more than 100. Her favourite is a metal heart. 'It shows me how much they love me,' she says.

## Vocabulary

**1** Put the words in the box in the correct columns.

summer  April  cold  field  fifth  autumn  first
flower  grass  hot  March  May  mountain  winter
ninth  October  second  spring  warm  wet

| Months | Ordinal numbers | Weather | Nature | Seasons |
|--------|-----------------|---------|--------|---------|
|        |                 |         |        |         |

76

**REVIEW and PRACTICE — 7 and 8**

**2** Circle the word that is different. Explain your answers.
1  artist     musician   winter    dancer
2  week      rain       month     year
3  beach     dry        sea       river
4  spring    summer     autumn    windy
5  snow      ride       sail      fly
6  foggy     sunny      sky       cloudy
7  forest    sixth      third     fourth
8  king      queen      tree      politician

**3** Choose the correct options to complete the sentences.
1  The summer in India is very _____ and wet.
   a hot        b sun         c cold
2  My sister _____ the train at King's Cross Station.
   a gets on    b gets in     c gets out
3  Don't _____ your bus! It leaves in five minutes.
   a take       b miss        c get lost
4  There are lots of big trees in this _____ .
   a flower     b foggy       c forest
5  Did you _____ your ticket to New York yesterday?
   a fly        b book        c sail
6  He _____ of the car at the police station.
   a got out    b got off     c got on
7  The _____ played the piano very well.
   a musician   b athlete     c dancer
8  It was a beautiful day, so we _____ to the park.
   a walked     b watched     c worked
9  With my smartphone, I never _____ in a new city.
   a miss       b get out     c get lost
10 You can't swim in the _____ . It's very dangerous.
   a river      b field       c sky

**4** Complete the sentences with the words in the box.

| ago  6.00  at (x2)  summer  in (x2) |
| Friday  last  on  yesterday  May |

1  I went to Greece _____ year on holiday.
2  Did you meet your friends on _____ ?
3  He started work _____ 7.00 this morning.
4  We usually go shopping _____ Saturday.
5  We can take the train at _____ .
6  His birthday is _____ June.
7  He started a new job two weeks _____ .
8  The first of _____ is a public holiday.
9  I played tennis with my brother _____ .
10 What did you do _____ the weekend?
11 She lived in Bogotá _____ 2016.
12 We didn't go on holiday in the _____ .

## Personal Best

**Lesson 7A** — Name five celebrities with different jobs.

**Lesson 8A** — List five irregular verbs and their past simple forms.

**Lesson 7A** — Write where you were on two different days last week.

**Lesson 8B** — Describe the weather in your favourite season.

**Lesson 7B** — Write the birthdays of four friends or family members.

**Lesson 8B** — Write three sentences with *quite, very* and *really* and an adjective.

**Lesson 7C** — Write three sentences beginning *Last year …, Two years ago …* and *Yesterday … .*

**Lesson 8C** — Name five things from nature you can see out of the window.

**Lesson 7C** — List five regular verbs and their past simple forms.

**Lesson 8C** — Write two sentences about your home as a child. Use *There was …* and *There were … .*

**Lesson 7D** — Describe what you did yesterday with *First, Then* and *After that.*

**Lesson 8D** — Write three sentences for buying a train ticket.

# UNIT 9

# Shopping

**LANGUAGE** present continuous ■ clothes

## 9A Street style

1 Match the words in the box with the clothes in the picture.

belt   jeans   jacket   T-shirt   hat

1 _____  2 _____  3 _____  4 _____  5 _____

Go to Vocabulary practice: clothes, page 128

2 Discuss the questions in pairs.
  1 What do you usually wear …
     a at home?   b at work/in class?   c on holiday?
  2 Where do you usually buy your clothes? What's your favourite shop?
  3 Do you buy second-hand clothes? Why/Why not?

3 Read the text and answer the questions.
  1 Where is Sukanya from?
  2 What type of clothes does she wear?
  3 Why does she buy these clothes?
  4 Where does she take Mark?

# Fashion Diary with Mark Ashcroft

This week, I'm in Thailand with local fashion blogger Sukanya Tanasan. Sukanya only wears second-hand clothes, but she looks amazing!
'There are some great places to buy clothes in Bangkok,' she says. 'If I need a new dress, a T-shirt or shoes, I always go to the markets. You can find really cool clothes there and they're cheap too!'
Today, Sukanya takes me to the Chatuchak market in Bangkok on a shopping trip.

 PLAY    DOWNLOAD

4 ▶9.2 Listen and tick (✓) the things Sukanya buys.
   T-shirt ☐   dress ☐   shoes ☐   hat ☐   skirt ☐

5 A ▶9.2 Complete the sentences with the words in the box. Listen again and check.

getting   buying   taking   eating   leaving   doing

  1 We're _____ the train to Chatuchak market.
  2 A lot of people are _____ out here.
  3 She's _____ the dress!
  4 What's this man _____ ?
  5 Sukanya, you aren't _____ the rice!
  6 We're _____ the market now.

B Look at sentences 1–6 again and answer the questions. Then read the Grammar box.
  1 What are the sentences about? *things happening now / regular events*
  2 Which three letters are at the end of the main verbs? _____
  3 Which verb do we use before the main verb? *be / do*

78

present continuous ■ clothes   LANGUAGE   **9A**

## Grammar present continuous

**Things that are happening now**

Positive:
I**'m going** to the market.
We**'re getting off** the bus.

Negative:
She **isn't having** a drink.
They **aren't wearing** glasses.

Questions and short answers:
**Are** you **working** today?
Yes, I **am**.   No, I**'m not**.

**Go to Grammar practice:** present continuous, page 104

**6** Complete the phone messages with the present continuous form of the verbs in brackets.

**7 A** ▶ 9.4 **Pronunciation:** -ing endings Listen and repeat. Pay attention to the /ɪŋ/ sound in **bold**.

com**ing**  go**ing**  do**ing**  runn**ing**  wait**ing**  stay**ing**

**B** ▶ 9.5 Say the questions and sentences. Then listen, check and repeat.

1 Where are you going?
2 She's running for her bus.
3 I'm not doing any work.
4 Are you staying?
5 He's coming to the café.
6 We're waiting for a taxi.

**Go to Communication practice:** Student A page 150, Student B page 149

**8** In pairs, ask and answer the question *What is/are ... doing?* about the people in the pictures.

**A** *What's David doing?*
**B** *I think he's having lunch in a restaurant.*

Hi Jorge, what ¹_____ you _____ (do)?
I ²_____ (go) to the town centre with Silvia.  11.35

Cool! I'm there too.  11.36

Do you want to have a coffee in 30 mins?
The café on Bridge Street?  11.36

11.37

I ³_____ (sit) next to the window.
Silvia ⁴_____ (not/stay). She needs to
buy a new dress. Are you here?  12.05

I ⁵_____ (get) a coffee.
Do you want one?  12.10

⁶_____ you _____ (come) ?!  12.19

Sorry. My battery died. I ⁷_____ (run)
to the café now.  12.25

Too late. We ⁸_____ (wait)
for the bus home.  12.26   12.26

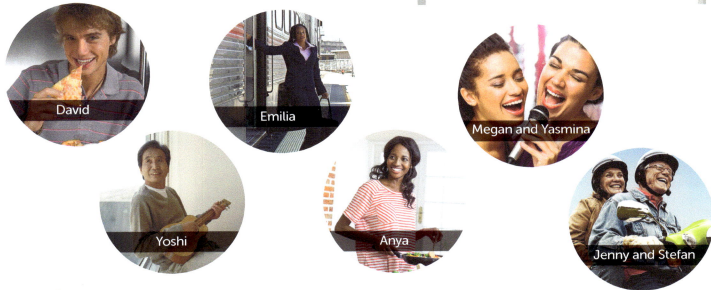

David   Emilia   Megan and Yasmina   Yoshi   Anya   Jenny and Stefan

**9** In pairs, describe a classmate. Your partner guesses the person.

**A** *She's wearing a blue dress and she's sitting next to Leon.*
**B** *Is it Malika?*
**A** *Yes, it is!*

**Personal Best**   Think of six people you know. Write sentences about what they're doing at the moment.

79

# 9 SKILLS  LISTENING  identifying key points ■ filler words ■ feelings

## 9B How do you feel?

**1** Match the words in the box with pictures a–f.

> angry   calm   excited   hungry   thirsty   tired

 a
 b
 c
 d
 e
 f

Go to Vocabulary practice: feelings, page 129

**2** ▶ 9.7   Complete the text with four feelings from exercise 1. Listen and check.

### Colours and feelings

Colours can sometimes change how we feel. For example, orange can make us feel happy and ¹_____ . A lot of restaurants, for example McDonald's and KFC, use red because it can make us feel ²_____ . Offices often use blue because it makes us ³_____ . But grey isn't a popular colour for offices because it can make us feel sad or ⁴_____ .

**3 A** Look at the picture of Ethan. How does his shirt make you feel?

**B** ▶ 9.8   Match the colours in the box with sentences 1–4. Watch or listen to the first part of *Learning Curve* and check.

> orange   blue   white   black   yellow

1 Doctors often wear this colour. _____
2 Firefighters usually wear these colours. _____ or _____
3 The police in the USA wear this colour. _____
4 People wear this colour when they're sad. _____

### 🔧 Skill   identifying key points

**When people speak, try to listen for the important things they say.**
- We often emphasize or repeat the most important ideas.
- We sometimes give examples or more information.

**4** ▶ 9.8   Read the Skill box. Then watch or listen again. Tick (✓) the **two** key points Ethan talks about.

a Colours can change how we feel. ☐
b Colours are important in festivals all around the world. ☐
c Orange is a popular colour for clothes. ☐
d Workers sometimes wear uniforms of the same colour. ☐

**5** Discuss the questions in pairs.

1 Do you wear a uniform for work?
2 Did you wear a uniform at school?
3 What colours are/were the uniforms?
4 How do/did they make you feel?

identifying key points ■ filler words ■ feelings    **LISTENING**    SKILLS    **9B**

**6** ▶9.9  Watch or listen to the rest of the show. Match the feelings in the box with the people.

bored   excited   scared   hungry   thirsty

1 _____    2 _____    3 _____    4 _____ and _____

**7** ▶9.9  Watch or listen again. Choose the correct options to complete the key points.

1 Udo _____ .
  a makes his own clothes    b buys expensive clothes    c only wears bright colours
2 Akiko _____ .
  a doesn't like *Learning Curve*    b doesn't like Ethan's shirt    c is late for class
3 Bob _____ .
  a loves the colour yellow    b wears a uniform for work    c wants to eat something

**8** Ask and answer the questions in the boxes.

What are you wearing today?   What colours are the clothes?   How do they make you feel?

**9** ▶9.10  Read the two extracts. Can you understand them without the missing words? Listen and write the missing words.

1 _____ Penny, what are people wearing today? Do you see a lot of colours on the streets of New York?

2 _____ , people are leaving work at the moment. Let's see what they're wearing.

---

**Listening builder**   filler words

When people speak, they often say short words while they are thinking of what to say. You can ignore these words – they don't really mean anything.
*So*, what are you, *er*, wearing today?
*Well*, I'm wearing blue jeans and, *um*, this red T-shirt.

---

**10** ▶9.11  Read the Listening builder. Then listen to the description of the photo. Tick (✓) the sentences the speaker says.

1 a This photo is of a young girl in a school. ☐
  b In this photo, there's a young girl at school. ☐
  c The photo shows a young girl in school. ☐
2 a And she's wearing a grey uniform and glasses. ☐
  b And she has a long grey uniform and glasses. ☐
  c And she's wearing a uniform and some glasses. ☐
3 a She's standing near the teacher's desk. ☐
  b In the class, there aren't any teachers. ☐
  c I think she's waiting for the teacher. ☐

**11** Discuss the questions in pairs.

1 What are your favourite colours?   3 Which colours don't you like?
2 How do they make you feel?         4 How do they make you feel?

**Personal Best**  Describe the colours in the rooms in your house and say how they make you feel.

# 9 LANGUAGE

*how often + expressions of frequency* ■ shopping

## 9C Love it or hate it?

**1** Complete phrases 1–5 with the words in the box.

buy   pay   shop   sell   try on

1 _____ shoes   2 _____ by credit card   3 _____ fruit   4 _____ online   5 _____ a new car

**Go to Vocabulary practice:** shopping, page 130

**2** Do the questionnaire in pairs. Write down your partner's answers. Then go to page 147 and look at the results.

## Shopping – do you love it or hate it?

**1 How often do you go to a shopping centre?**
a Never! I hate shopping centres.
b I only go when I need some new clothes.
c I go there every week. I love it!

**2 Do you spend a lot of money on clothes and shoes?**
a No, I don't. I usually buy second-hand clothes.
b When I have a special occasion – once or twice a year.
c Yes, I do. Clothes are very important to me.

**3 How often do you shop online?**
a Not often. Maybe once a year.
b A few times a month.
c Very often. Three or four times a week.

**4 How do you feel if you need to buy a present for someone?**
a Bored. I prefer to give cash as a present.
b Happy. I can find something in a local shop.
c Really excited! I can go shopping all day on Saturday!

**5 How do you usually pay when you go shopping?**
a I pay with cash. I never spend money that I don't have.
b I sometimes pay with cash and sometimes by card.
c I usually pay by credit card.

**3 A** Complete the questions and sentences from the questionnaire with the words in the box.

how   every   times   twice   often   once

1 How _____ do you go to a shopping centre?
2 I go there _____ week.
3 Once or _____ a year.
4 _____ often do you shop online?
5 Maybe _____ a year.
6 Three or four _____ a week.

**B** Which tense do we use to talk about the frequency of events? *present simple / present continuous*
Read the Grammar box.

82

how often + expressions of frequency ■ shopping    LANGUAGE   9C

### Grammar  how often + expressions of frequency

**How often** do you go shopping?

| I go shopping | once a<br>twice a<br>three/four times a<br>every | day/week/month/year. |

Go to Grammar practice: *how often + expressions of frequency, page 104*

**4  A** ▶ 9.14  **Pronunciation:** sentence stress  Listen and repeat the expressions of frequency. Pay attention to the underlined stressed words.

1  <u>once</u> a <u>day</u>
2  <u>twice</u> a <u>year</u>
3  <u>three</u> <u>times</u> a <u>month</u>
4  <u>every</u> <u>day</u> and <u>every</u> <u>night</u>

**B** ▶ 9.15  Say the sentences. Pay attention to the sentence stress. Listen, check and repeat.

1  I call my girlfriend twice a day.
2  We go to the cinema every month.
3  They shop online three times a week.
4  My grandparents visit every year.

Go to Communication practice: *Student A page 141, Student B page 149*

**5  A** Write the questions.

1  How often / you buy someone a present?
_____
_____
_____

4  How often / it snow in your town?
_____
_____
_____

2  How often / your teacher give homework?
_____
_____
_____

5  How often / you go to bed after midnight?
_____
_____
_____

3  How often / you wash your hair?
_____
_____
_____

6  How often / you pay by credit card?
_____
_____
_____

**B** In pairs, ask and answer the questions.

A  *How often do you buy someone a present?*
B  *I buy someone a present once or twice a month. How about you?*

**6  A** Write three true sentences and three false sentences about you with expressions of frequency.
**B** Read your sentences to your partner. Guess if they are true or false.

A  *I go to Singapore twice a year.*
B  *I think that's false.*
A  *No, it's true! My sister lives there.*

**Personal Best**  Write some more questions about shopping for a questionnaire.

## 9 SKILLS  WRITING  describing a photo ■ describing position

## 9D Garage sale

**1 A** What do you do with things you don't use any more?

a  Throw them away.
b  Take them to a second-hand shop.
c  Sell them online.
d  Have a garage sale.

**B** Discuss the questions in pairs.
1 How often do you buy second-hand things?
2 What type of second-hand things do you buy?
3 Do people have garage sales in your country?
4 Do you think they're a good idea? Why/Why not?

**2 A** Read the email quickly. What relationship is the writer to Patrick?

**B** Read the email again. Match the names in the box with the people in the picture.

Bill   Sandra   Evie   Eddie

Hi Patrick,

How are you?

a  We had a garage sale yesterday. It was at our house and we sold some old clothes, books and other things.

b  Here's a photo. The man on the right is our friend, Bill. He's looking at our old things. His wife Sandra is on the left, and the girl in the middle is their daughter, Evie. She's trying on my old hat. There's an old skateboard at the bottom of the photo – I think it's your dad's. The man at the top of the picture is our neighbour, Eddie. He's looking at a pair of Grandpa's old trousers!

c  We made about £100! We bought some new chairs for the garden with the money.

Email me soon with your news.

Grandma

**3 A** Match paragraphs a–c with the parts of the email 1–3.
1 description of photo ____
2 what happened after ____
3 introduction ____

**B** What tenses are the verbs in paragraphs a–c? Read the Skill box.

### Skill  describing a photo

When we describe a photo, we:
- explain who the people are: *The man on the right is our friend, Bill.*
- use the present continuous to say what they are doing: *She's trying on my old hat.*
- use *there is/are* to say what things are in the picture: *There's an old skateboard ...*

84

describing a photo ■ describing position   **WRITING**   **SKILLS**   **9D**

**4** Complete Patrick's reply with the correct form of the verbs in brackets.

Dear Grandma,

I'm very well, thanks. That's great about the garage sale!

I ¹_____ (go) to Bristol last Saturday with some friends. We ²_____ (take) the train in the morning and we ³_____ (explore) the city.

Here's a photo. The girl on the left is Sara and the girl in the middle is Lisa. They ⁴_____ (be) my classmates from university. They ⁵_____ (try) to find the Clifton Suspension Bridge on the map. Lisa's boyfriend, Shaun, is on the right. He ⁶_____ (take) a photo of some street art.

It was a fun day out, but we ⁷_____ (be) all really tired when we ⁸_____ (get) home!

Love Patrick x

**5** Match the halves to make sentences. Check your answers in the emails.

1 The man on
2 The girl in
3 There's an old skateboard at
4 The man at
5 The girl on

a the left is Sara.
b the middle is their daughter, Evie.
c the right is our friend, Bill.
d the top of the picture is our neighbour, Eddie.
e the bottom of the photo.

### Text builder   describing position

◆ on the right      ◆ at the top        ✕ in the middle
◆ on the left       ◆ at the bottom     ◣ in the corner

**6 A** Read the Text builder. Then write sentences.
1 that / my brother / right     _That's my brother on the right._
2 my friend Casey / middle      _____
3 there / a cat / corner        _____
4 that / my cousin / top        _____
5 there / more people / left    _____

**B** In pairs, take a photo of some of your classmates. Describe the photo using phrases from the Text builder.

*That's Nacho on the left and Lourdes is on the right. There's a blue bag in the corner. It's Nacho's bag.*

**7 A PREPARE** Choose one of the photos. Imagine that you took it. Make notes to answer the questions.

1 When and where did you take the photo?
2 Who are the people in the photo?
3 What are they doing?
4 What happened after you took the photo?

**B PRACTISE** Write an email. Introduce the photo, describe it and say what happened after you took it.

**C PERSONAL BEST** Swap emails with your partner and read it. Check the tenses of the verbs and prepositions for describing position. Can you improve anything?

**Personal Best**   Write an email describing one of your own photos.

85

# UNIT 10 Time out

**LANGUAGE** present continuous for future plans ■ free-time activities

## 10A What are you doing at the weekend?

**1 A** Look at the poster for a music festival. Discuss the questions in pairs.
1. Do you know this music festival?
2. Where and when is the festival?
3. Do you like music festivals? Why/Why not?
4. What can you see in the pictures?

**B** Complete the text with the words in the box.

visit   go   watch   have   stay

**COACHELLA** Music and Arts **Festival**

**Win tickets** for an incredible Coachella experience

Call 08081 570000 and tell us why you want to go.

1 _____ to all the concerts
2 _____ in a luxury tent
3 _____ the art area and see amazing sculptures
4 _____ films at night
5 _____ a good time!

April 14–16
Coachella Valley, California

Go to Vocabulary practice: free-time activities, page 131

**2** ▶ 10.2 Read and listen to the conversation between two friends. Where is Alex going this weekend?

**Alex** Guess what I'm doing this weekend.
**Dan** I don't know. Are you visiting your family again?
**Alex** No, I'm not. I'm going to a music festival – Coachella! I won tickets in a competition.
**Dan** Coachella? No way! Which bands are playing?
**Alex** Radiohead are playing on Friday and Lady Gaga on Saturday.
**Dan** That's amazing. Are you going on your own?
**Alex** No, the prize was for two tickets.
**Dan** Two tickets? You know, I'm not doing anything this weekend …
**Alex** Sorry, Dan. I'm going with my mother.
**Dan** Your mother?
**Alex** Yeah, she loves Lady Gaga. We're driving there tonight and then we're staying in a tent all weekend!
**Dan** Well, have a good time. Tell me all about it on Monday, OK?

**3** Are the sentences true (T) or false (F)? Check your answers in the conversation.

1 Dan's going to Coachella with Alex. ____
2 Lady Gaga's playing on Saturday. ____
3 They're driving to the festival tonight. ____
4 They're staying in a hotel all weekend. ____

present continuous for future plans ■ free-time activities    LANGUAGE  10A

**4 A** Look at the sentences in exercise 3 again. Answer the questions.
1 Which tense are the verbs? *present simple / past simple / present continuous*
2 When do the actions happen? *in the past / now / in the future*

**B** Find more examples of this tense in the conversation in exercise 2. Then read the Grammar box.

### Grammar — present continuous for future plans

**Positive:**
I'**m going** to a music festival this weekend.
We'**re visiting** a museum tomorrow.

**Negative:**
Sue **isn't going** to the concert tonight.
They **aren't staying** in a hotel.

**Questions and short answers:**
**Are** you **having** a party in the summer?
Yes, I **am**.  No, I'**m not**.

Go to Grammar practice: present continuous for future plans, page 105

**5 A** ▶10.5 **Pronunciation:** sentence stress Listen and repeat the questions and answers from the conversation in exercise 2. Pay attention to the underlined stressed words.
1 Are you <u>visiting</u> your <u>family</u>?   <u>No</u>, I'm <u>not</u>.
2 <u>Which</u> <u>bands</u> are <u>playing</u>?   <u>Radiohead</u> are <u>playing</u> on <u>Friday</u>.

**B** ▶10.6  Match the questions with answers a–c. Ask and answer the questions in pairs with the correct stress. Listen, check and repeat.
1 What are you doing this weekend?     a I'm taking the bus.
2 How are you getting there?           b Yes, I am.
3 Are you staying with friends?        c I'm going to the beach.

**6** Look at Rosie's diary on her smartphone. In pairs, ask and answer the question *What's she doing …?* with the times in the box.

> ~~this morning~~   on Friday   tomorrow   at the weekend
> the day after tomorrow   this evening

**A** *What's she doing this morning?*
**B** *She's having coffee with Kate.*

**Go to Communication practice:**
Student A page 141, Student B page 149

**7 A** ▶10.7  Use the words to write questions in the present continuous. Listen to the conversation and check.
1 What / you / do / at the weekend?
_____
2 Who / you / go / with?
_____
3 How / you / get / there?
_____
4 When / you / leave?
_____
5 Where / you / stay?
_____

**B** ▶10.7  Listen again and write Cheryl's answers to the questions.

**8 A** Make notes about your plans for the weekend. They can be real or imaginary.
**B** In pairs, ask and answer the questions in exercise 7 about your plans.

**A** *What are you doing at the weekend?*   **B** *I'm having a barbecue with my friends.*

**Personal Best**   Write a paragraph about your 'perfect' weekend.

Rosie's diary:
< May
Tuesday 6 (today)
11:00 Coffee with Kate
19:30 Cinema with Malika
Wednesday 7
11.15 Meet Sandra
Thursday 8
14:00 Picasso exhibition
Friday 9
20:00 My party!
Saturday 10
10:30 Visit Mum and Dad
View Today   Inbox (4)

# 10 SKILLS    READING    scanning for information ■ the imperative ■ types of music and film

## 10B What's on?

**1** ▶ 10.8 Listen and match the words in the box with the types of music and film.

classical  science-fiction  action  jazz  electronic  romance

1 _____  2 _____  3 _____  4 _____  5 _____  6 _____

Go to Vocabulary practice: types of music and film, page 132

**2** Look at the webpage on page 89. What type of website is it? Do you use websites like this?

### Skill    scanning for information

'Scanning' means looking quickly at a text to find specific information.
- Underline the key word(s) in the question.
- Look for the word(s) in the text quickly. Use your finger to help you.
- When you find the word, read the information to answer the question.

**3 A** Read the Skill box. Then read questions 1–4 and scan the text for the answers. The key words are underlined.

1 What time does the concert start?  _____
2 Where is the art exhibition?  _____
3 How much is a cinema ticket for children?  _____
4 Which event is free to enter?  _____

**B** Read questions 1–4 and underline the key words. Then scan the text for the answers.

1 What's the name of the theatre in the city?  _____
2 How old do you need to be to try speed dating?  _____
3 Which event costs less if you buy tickets online?  _____
4 Who's playing electronic music tonight?  _____

**4** Look at the text and discuss the questions in pairs.

1 Which events do you want to go to? Why?
2 Which events aren't you interested in? Why?

**5** Complete the sentences from the text with the correct words.

1 Don't _____ it!
2 _____ to our Speed Dating night!
3 _____ all night.
4 _____ very scared!

### Text builder    the imperative

We use the imperative to give instructions.
**Book** early!  **Open** the window!  **Don't be** late!  **Don't forget** about the party!

**6** Read the Text builder. Then complete the sentences with the positive or negative imperative of the verbs in the box.

call  listen  talk  sit  open  be

1 _____ down, please. I can't see the film.
2 The concert starts at 7.45, so _____ late.
3 _____ to this great song. I love it!
4 _____ the window, please. It's very hot.
5 Please _____ in the library. I'm trying to read.
6 _____ me today because I'm working.

**7** Discuss the questions in pairs.

1 What's your favourite type of music?
2 When do you listen to music?
3 How often do you go to concerts/nightclubs?
4 What type of films do you like?
5 What was the last film you saw?
6 How often do you go to the cinema?

scanning for information ■ the imperative ■ types of music and film   READING   SKILLS   10B

# What's On

**Events in your area:** Saturday 9 June    Sort by: Date

### Visitors
Science-fiction adventure. When aliens arrive on Earth, do they want to help people – or start a war?
ABC Cinema, 6.30 p.m. 9.00 p.m. 11.30 p.m.
Tickets £10. Under-16s: £8

🎟 Buy Tickets

### Anderson .Paak in concert
Anderson .Paak brings his mix of jazz, hip-hop and rock to the city. Don't miss it!
Royal Arena, 8.00 p.m.
Tickets £17.50

🎟 Sold Out

### Romeo and Juliet
William Shakespeare's great love story. A boy and a girl find love on the streets of Verona.
King's Theatre, 7.15 p.m.
Tickets £18.00

🎟 Sold Out

### Underwater garden
Dance all night as DJ Octopus plays the latest in electronic music from around the world.
Club Infinity, 10.00 p.m.–late          Entry £8.00 (Over-18s only)

🎟 Buy Tickets

### Hot Potato
Enjoy an evening of comedy with Sally Quentin. 'Really funny' *The Daily Times*. Book online and save £5.
Comedy Club, 7.00 p.m.
Tickets £15 on the door

🎟 Buy Tickets

### Looking for love?
Are you single? Do you want to find that special person? Come to our Speed Dating night – the fun way to meet new people!
Union Café, 6.30 p.m.
Admission £15. Minimum age 21

🎟 Buy Tickets

### Book reading with Joe Arnott
Joe Arnott reads from his new horror story, *Play With Fire*. Be scared, be very scared!
Forest Hill Library, 8.00 p.m.
Admission free. Over-16s only.

🎟 Reserve

### Picasso's portraits
Exhibition of paintings and sculptures from one of the most popular artists of the twentieth century.
Trinidad Gallery
Tickets £12.50

🎟 Buy Tickets

**Personal Best** — Write information about three events in your town or city. Use imperatives.

# 10 LANGUAGE question review ■ sports and games

## 10C Royal hobbies

**1** Complete the sports and games with the verbs *go*, *play* and *do*.

1 _____ tennis   2 _____ karate   3 _____ running   4 _____ rock climbing   5 _____ videogames   6 _____ yoga

Go to Vocabulary practice: sports and games, page 133

**2** In pairs, ask and answer the question *Do you ...?* with the correct verbs and the sports and games in the box.

A *Do you go cycling?*   B *Yes, I do. I usually go cycling once a week.*

cycling   swimming   football   Pilates   gymnastics   basketball   chess   karate   skiing

**3 A** Who are the people in the picture? Read the text and check. What do you know about them?

**B** ▶10.11 Guess which three activities in exercise 1 the people do. Listen to the interview and check.

**4 A** ▶10.11 Complete the interviewer's questions with the words in the box. Listen again and check.

was   where   how   does   is   what

1 _____ does he relax?
2 _____ is his favourite game?
3 _____ did she go to university?
4 _____ she good at sports?
5 _____ William do lots of exercise too?
6 _____ he training for a marathon now?

**B** Look at questions 1–6 again.
1 Which questions do you answer with *yes* or *no*? ____ ____ ____
2 Which questions do you answer with specific information? ____ ____ ____

7.00 p.m.
**Relaxing with the Royals**

What do Prince Harry, Prince William and his wife Kate, the Duchess of Cambridge, do in their free time? Royal expert Jenny Brown joins us to talk about how the young royals relax.

**5 A** Match the tenses in the box with the questions in 4A.

past simple   present continuous   present simple (x2)   present simple of *be*   past simple of *be*

1 _____ 2 _____ 3 _____ 4 _____ 5 _____ 6 _____

**B** Match the words in the box with the parts of the question 1–4. Then read the Grammar box.

subject   question word   main verb   auxiliary verb

1 What _____ 2 do _____ 3 they _____ 4 do _____ in their free time?

question review ■ sports and games     **LANGUAGE  10C**

📖 **Grammar**  question review

**Most verbs:** (question word) + auxiliary verb + subject + main verb:
Where do you live?   What are you doing?   When did they arrive?
Does Carla play tennis?   Is he watching TV?   Did you go running yesterday?

**The verb *be*:** (question word) + *be* + subject:
How old are you?   Where was Antonio yesterday?
Is the milk in the fridge?   Were you worried about the exam?

Go to Grammar practice: question review, page 105

**6  A**  ▶ 10.14  **Pronunciation:** Intonation in questions  Listen and repeat the questions. Pay attention to the intonation that goes up (↗) or down (↘).

questions with question words          yes/no questions
1 Which films do you like? ↘           3 Is she from Japan? ↗
2 Where are they going? ↘              4 Did you stay in a hotel? ↗

**B**  ▶ 10.15  Say the questions with the correct intonation. Listen, check and repeat. Then ask and answer the questions in pairs.

1 What are you doing tonight?          4 How often do you take the bus?
2 Did you cook dinner yesterday?       5 Is it raining at the moment?
3 Where were you at 7.00 this morning? 6 Does our teacher like pop music?

Go to Communication practice: Student A page 141, Student B page 150

**7  A**  ▶ 10.16  Order the words to make questions 1–6. Listen and check.
**B**  ▶ 10.16  In pairs, ask and answer the questions. Listen again and check.

| Estonian fashion model Carmen Kass plays chess. | American singer Elvis Presley did karate. | American actor Lucy Liu goes rock climbing. |
|---|---|---|
| 1 start / did / when / she _____? | 3 karate / at / was / good / he _____? | 5 go / how / rock climbing / she / does / often _____? |
| 2 she / how / did / learn _____? | 4 where / do / did / it / he _____? | 6 dangerous / is / it _____? |

**8**  Choose a sport or game that you do. In pairs, ask and answer the questions in the boxes.

- What's your hobby?
- When did you start?
- Where do you do it?
- How often do you do it?
- Are you doing it this weekend?
- Is it difficult?
- Is it expensive?
- How did you learn?
- Who do you do it with?
- What do you need to do it?

**Personal Best**  Write a paragraph about a sport or game you enjoy.

**SKILLS** — SPEAKING — showing interest ■ asking about a tourist attraction

## 10D  Where are we going now?

**1** Look at the pictures and answer the questions.
1. Which tourist attractions can you see?
2. Which countries are they in?
3. Do you want to visit them? Why/Why not?
4. What tourist attractions are there in your town/city?

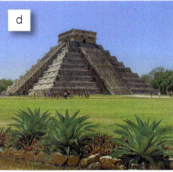

**2 A** ▶ 10.17  Watch or listen to the first part of *Learning Curve*. Where is Ethan? Who does he meet?

**B** ▶ 10.17  Choose the correct options to complete the sentences. Watch or listen again and check.

1. Flushing Meadows is famous for its *football stadium / tennis stadium*.
2. There were two World's Fairs in the park – in 1939 and in *1964 / 1974*.
3. There is a *science museum / design museum* in the park.
4. Ethan, Penny and Taylor are meeting Marc in *half an hour / an hour*.
5. Marc and Taylor *know / don't know* each other.

**3** ▶ 10.18  Listen and complete the questions in the conversation.

**Taylor**  So what time ¹_____ the Hall of Science _____ ?
**Ethan**  It opens at 10.00 a.m.
**Penny**  What ²_____ _____ to do if it rains?
**Ethan**  Well, we can stay inside and look at exhibits all day.
**Penny**  OK. Sounds good. When ³_____ it _____ ?
**Ethan**  6.00 p.m.
**Taylor**  OK, great. So, what ⁴_____ we _____ now?
**Ethan**  We're meeting our friend Marc from *Learning Curve*, at the Information Desk.

| **Conversation builder** | **asking about a tourist attraction** |
|---|---|

*What time does it open/close?*   *Is there a café/restaurant/gift shop?*
*Which days is it open?*           *What is there to do if it rains?*
*How do you get there?*            *Are there any special events?*

**4 A** Read the Conversation builder. Then look at the information about a tourist attraction on page 93. Ask and answer questions in pairs.

**A** *What time does it open?*      **B** *It opens at 9.30 a.m.*

**B** Do you want to visit this attraction? Why/Why not?

showing interest ■ asking about a tourist attraction  **SPEAKING**  **SKILLS 10D**

# Fun days out  Legoland > Plan your trip    Week: 13–19 September

| Monday | Tuesday | Wednesday | Thursday | Friday | Saturday | Sunday |

● 9.30 a.m. – 5.00 p.m. (£30)   ● 9.30 a.m. – 6.00 p.m. (£35)   ● Closed

**Weather:** Most attractions are outside. Umbrellas are available from the gift shop. Inside attractions include: LEGO 4D Movie Theatre, Imagination Centre and the Exploratorium workshops.

**Food & drink:** City Walk Pizza and Pasta, Hill Top Café and many more.

**Getting there:**
By car: Legoland is on the B3022 road (parking available).
By bus: Take the number 200 bus from Windsor Theatre Royal.

31 December: Kids' New Year's Eve firework show

**5 A** ▶ 10.19  Watch or listen to the second part of the show. How many exhibits do Penny, Marc, Ethan and Taylor see in the Hall of Science?

**B** ▶ 10.19  Are the sentences true (T) or false (F)? Watch or listen again and check.

1 Tickets for the Hall of Science cost $15.  ____
2 There are almost 450 exhibits.  ____
3 Marc and Ethan buy tickets for a 3D film.  ____
4 Taylor doesn't like flying.  ____
5 Taylor wants a flying car.  ____
6 They decide to eat pizza.  ____

Penny   Ethan   Marc   Taylor

**6** ▶ 10.20  Match the sentences with the responses. Listen, check and repeat the responses.

1 It costs $15, but we paid for you.
2 What about *Journey into Space*? It's a 3D film.
3 We're hungry and we're eating a very large pizza.

a OK. Sounds good.
b Oh really? Thanks!
c That sounds interesting.

### Skill   showing interest

When people speak to you, it's important to show that you're listening.
• Use expressions: *Oh really? That sounds good. Great.*
• Use intonation to sound interested.

**7 A** ▶ 10.21  Read the Skill box. Then listen to conversations 1–4. Which response sounds more interested: *a* or *b*?

1 I'm visiting my family this weekend.  ____
2 My sister goes rock climbing every week.  ____
3 There's a new comedy at the cinema.  ____
4 We went to the beach yesterday.  ____

**B** ▶ 10.22  Listen and repeat the interested responses.

**Go to Communication practice:** Students A and B, page 150

**8 A PREPARE** In pairs, invent a tourist attraction and write information about it. Include:
• the days and times it is open
• the price of tickets
• what you can do
• how to get there
• shops and restaurants
• special events

**B PRACTISE** Swap your information with another pair. Then ask and answer questions about the tourist attraction. Remember to show you're interested.

A *What time does the museum open?*   B *It opens at 9.30 a.m.*   A *OK, great.*

**C PERSONAL BEST** Listen to the other pair. Do they ask questions well? Do they show interest?

**Personal Best**   Write about a tourist attraction in your town/city.

93

## 9 and 10 REVIEW and PRACTICE

## Grammar

**1** Tick (✓) the correct sentences.

1. a  I can't talk now. I'm doing my homework.
   b  I can't talk now. I do my homework.
   c  I can't talk now. I did my homework.
2. a  They not working at the moment.
   b  They aren't working at the moment.
   c  They don't working at the moment.
3. a  What often do you go to the gym?
   b  How often do you go to the gym?
   c  How much often do you go to the gym?
4. a  I see my brother three times at year.
   b  I see my brother three times for year.
   c  I see my brother three times a year.
5. a  What are you doing tomorrow?
   b  What do you do tomorrow?
   c  What you are doing tomorrow?
6. a  He not is coming to the party tonight.
   b  He isn't coming to the party tonight.
   c  He doesn't come to the party tonight.
7. a  What time did the train leave?
   b  What time the train did leave?
   c  What time left the train?
8. a  They were at work yesterday.
   b  Did they be at work yesterday?
   c  Were they at work yesterday?

**2** Complete the questions and sentences with the correct form of the verbs in the box.

> cost  finish  spend  go  have  meet
> not be  not study  can buy  wear

1. How often _____ you _____ a shower?
2. Carlos _____ some new boots today. Look – they're really nice.
3. What time _____ you _____ work last night?
4. We _____ shopping in London next Tuesday.
5. How much _____ your new coat _____ ? Was it expensive?
6. She's in the library, but she _____ . She's texting a friend.
7. _____ you _____ your friends next weekend?
8. He _____ at work yesterday. I think he was ill.
9. Where _____ I _____ some good shoes?
10. How much money _____ you _____ on clothes every month?

**3** Complete the text with the correct form of the verbs in brackets.

### The Kinderkook Café

**The Kinderkook Café** in Amsterdam is a café with a difference – the chefs and waiters are all children! Parents take their children to the café in the afternoon and the children cook a meal. Then, in the evening, the parents return to eat it. Matt Baker talked to one of the parents, Sonja Kroes.

| | |
|---|---|
| Matt | When ¹_____ the café _____ (start)? |
| Sonja | It started in 1981. It's very popular. |
| Matt | What ²_____ the children _____ (cook)? |
| Sonja | They cook pasta, curry, pizza and lots more. The food is healthy and delicious. |
| Matt | How often ³_____ you _____ (come) here with your daughter? |
| Sonja | We come once a month. Lotte loves it! |
| Matt | ⁴_____ she _____ (work) here today? |
| Sonja | Yes, she is. She ⁵_____ (make) a cake. Look, she's over there. She ⁶_____ (wear) a pink jumper. And her friend, Stijn, is helping her. They ⁷_____ (have) a good time! |
| Matt | ⁸_____ you _____ (eat) here tonight? |
| Sonja | Yes, I am. I ⁹_____ (come) with my husband and my parents. It was Lotte's birthday yesterday, and she wanted to have a small party here with the family. |
| Matt | That's nice. How old ¹⁰_____ (be) she? |
| Sonja | She's seven. |

## Vocabulary

**1** Put the words in the box in the correct columns.

> volleyball  a museum  videogames  an art gallery
> a suit  shopping  cycling  gymnastics  karate
> trousers  walking  tennis  yoga  my family  a belt

| go | do | visit | wear | play |
|---|---|---|---|---|
| | | | | |

94

**REVIEW and PRACTICE 9 and 10**

**2** Circle the word that is different. Explain your answers.
1 angry    happy       hockey       thirsty
2 skirt    beach       jacket       dress
3 festival concert     suit         party
4 tent     pay         spend        buy
5 pop      rock        jazz         coat
6 socks    boots       shoes        trousers
7 museum   art gallery jumper       department store
8 money    comedy      romance      drama

**3** Choose the correct options to complete the sentences.
1 Can I try _____ this shirt, please?
  a in         b off         c on
2 That shop _____ really nice T-shirts.
  a sells      b spends      c pays
3 Let's stay _____ home tonight. I'm really tired.
  a in         b at          c on
4 Do you want to _____ a video?
  a go         b look        c watch
5 I don't have any money. Can I pay _____ card?
  a with       b by          c for
6 I usually shop _____ . I don't have time to go to the supermarket.
  a online     b by card     c by cash
7 We're _____ a barbecue at the weekend. Would you like to come?
  a having     b staying     c spending
8 We don't accept credit cards here. Can you pay with _____ , please?
  a chess      b cash        c calm

**4** Complete the conversation with the words in the box.

hungry   excited   time   scared
horror   bored    happy   tired

**Bella** What did you do last night, Ruby?
**Ruby** Tim and I went to the cinema. We watched that new ¹_____ film, *Black Night*.
**Bella** Were you ²_____ ?
**Ruby** No, we were ³_____ . It wasn't very good.
**Bella** That's a pity. Did you do anything after the film?
**Ruby** We were really ⁴_____ , so we went to a restaurant.
**Bella** How was the food?
**Ruby** It was excellent, so we were ⁵_____ ! What about you? What did you do?
**Bella** We went to a concert – the Foo Fighters. They're Nick's favourite band. He was very ⁶_____ when he got tickets.
**Ruby** Did you have a good ⁷_____ ?
**Bella** Yes, it was great. The concert finished at 1.00 in the morning, so I'm really ⁸_____ today!

# Personal Best

**Lesson 9A** Name five types of clothes.

**Lesson 10A** Name three activities a tourist can do in your town or city.

**Lesson 9A** Write what three friends or family members are doing now.

**Lesson 10A** Write about your plans for two days next week. Use the present continuous.

**Lesson 9B** Name three positive feelings.

**Lesson 10B** Write three instructions using the imperative.

**Lesson 9C** Write a sentence about shopping.

**Lesson 10C** Name six sports or games. Use the verbs *go*, *play* and *do*.

**Lesson 9C** Write three questions with *How often …?* Then answer the questions.

**Lesson 10C** Write questions with *What*, *When* and *Where* in three different tenses.

**Lesson 9D** Describe a photo on your phone or in a magazine.

**Lesson 10D** Write three questions to ask about a tourist attraction.

95

## GRAMMAR PRACTICE

### Hello  The verb *be* (*I, you*)

We use the verb *be* to give information about people.

*I'm Carlos and I'm a teacher.*

We usually use contractions in positive and negative forms.

*You're a student.* = You are a student.
*I'm not in Class 3.* = I am not in Class 3.

| ▶ 1.4 | I | you |
|---|---|---|
| + | I'm a student. | You're a teacher. |
| – | I'm not a teacher. | You aren't a student. |
| ? | Am I in Class 2? | Are you in my class? |
| Y/N | Yes, I am. / No, I'm not. | Yes, you are. / No, you aren't. |

### 1A  The verb *be* (*he, she, it*)

We use *he*, *she* and *it* to talk about a person or a thing.

*The teacher is Mexican. He's from Puebla.*
*The car isn't from Germany. It's from Japan.*

We usually use contractions in positive and negative forms.

*Akemi isn't Chinese.* = Akemi is not Chinese.
*She's Japanese.* = She is Japanese.

| ▶ 1.14 | he | she | it |
|---|---|---|---|
| + | Leo's from Peru. | Lucía's Colombian. | The book's Chinese. |
| – | He isn't from Chile. | She isn't Argentinian. | It isn't Italian. |
| ? | Is Ravi from India? | Is Ayla Turkish? | Is the car German? |
| Y/N | Yes, he is. / No, he isn't. | Yes, she is. / No, she isn't. | Yes, it is. / No, it isn't. |

### 1C  The verb *be* (*we, you, they*)

We use *we*, *you* and *they* to talk about people and things in the plural.

*The engineers are here. They're from India.*
*Susan and I aren't happy. We're sad.*

We usually use contractions in positive and negative forms.

*You're in Class 3.* = You are in Class 3.
*The pizzas aren't expensive.* = The pizzas are not expensive.

| ▶ 1.29 | we | you | they |
|---|---|---|---|
| + | We're 25 years old. | You're doctors. | They're French. |
| – | We aren't old. | You aren't chefs. | Ana and Bea aren't here. |
| ? | Are we sad? | Are you happy? | Are they in Class 4? |
| Y/N | Yes, we are. / No, we aren't. | Yes, you are. / No, you aren't. | Yes, they are. / No, they aren't. |

---

1 Choose the correct words to complete the sentences and questions.

1 I *'m* / *'re* Harry.
2 You *'m* / *'re* Lola.
3 *Am* / *Are* you a student?
4 *Am I* / *I'm* in Room 3.
5 *Are you* / *You are* late?
6 No, I *'m not* / *aren't*.
7 *Am* / *Are* I in this class?
8 Yes, you *am* / *are*.

◀ Go back to page 4

1 Complete the sentences with the correct words.

1 This is my friend Daniel. He _____ from Spain.
2 Anna isn't in class today. _____'s at home.
3 Sophie _____ a student. She's the teacher.
4 This is my car. _____'s a Toyota.
5 A Where _____ Leonardo DiCaprio from?
  B He _____ from the USA.
6 A What's the capital of Australia? Is _____ Sydney?
  B No, it _____ . It's Canberra.
7 A _____ María from Colombia?
  B No, she _____ . She's from Mexico.
8 A Is sushi from Japan?
  B Yes, _____ is.

◀ Go back to page 7

1 Rewrite the sentences. Change the words in **bold** to *we*, *you* or *they*.

1 **Elsa and Lucy** are police officers.
   _____
2 **Maite and I** are 21 years old.
   _____
3 Are **you and Wei** from China?
   _____
4 **The doctors** aren't from India.
   _____
5 Where are **Maggie and Jake Gyllenhaal** from?
   _____
6 How old are **you and your friend**?
   _____

2 Choose the correct words to complete the questions and sentences.

1 We *isn't* / *aren't* doctors.
2 *Is* / *Are* Ismail from Turkey?
3 Sam and I *am* / *are* in London.
4 I *'m not* / *aren't* your teacher.
5 Where *is* / *are* the actor from?
6 Ana and Rosa *is* / *are* from Spain.

◀ Go back to page 11

GRAMMAR PRACTICE

## 2A Singular and plural nouns

We use *a* and *an* with singular nouns. We use *a* with nouns that start with consonants (*b*, *d*, *f*, *g*, etc.) and we use *an* with nouns that start with vowels (*a*, *e*, *i*, *o*, *u*).

*It's a book.*   *She's an actor.*

To make a noun plural, we usually add *-s* or *-es*.

*a key* ⇨ *three keys*   *a watch* ⇨ *two watches*

▶ 2.3

| Singular | Plural |
|---|---|
| It's **an** umbrella. | They're umbrella**s**. |
| I'm **a** waitress. | We're waitress**es**. |

**Spelling rules for plurals**

We usually add *-s* to nouns to make a plural.
*bag* ⇨ *bags*

When a noun ends in a consonant + *y*, we remove the *y* and then add *-ies*.
*country* ⇨ *countries*

When a noun ends in *ch*, *sh*, *s* or *x*, we add *-es*.
*watch* ⇨ *watches*

Some plurals are irregular.
*child* ⇨ *children*   *man* ⇨ *men*   *woman* ⇨ *women*   *person* ⇨ *people*

1 Complete the sentences with singular or plural nouns and *a* or *an*, if necessary.

| Singular | Plural |
|---|---|
| 1 It's a city. | They're _____ . |
| 2 She's _____ . | They're actors. |
| 3 Are you a waitress? | Are you _____ ? |
| 4 He isn't _____ . | They aren't children. |
| 5 It's a watch. | They're _____ . |
| 6 It isn't _____ . | They aren't umbrellas. |
| 7 I'm a woman. | We're _____ . |
| 8 He's _____ . | They're people. |

2 Match the parts to make sentences and questions.

1 Alice is an _____     a tour guide.
2 It's an _____          b IT worker.
3 He's a _____           c umbrella.
4 Jo and I are _____     d engineers.
5 Are you a _____        e sunglasses?
6 Where are my _____     f chef?

◀ Go back to page 14

## 2A this, that, these, those

We use *this* and *these* + the verb *be* to identify things that are near us.

*This is my bag and these are my sunglasses.*

We use *that* and *those* + the verb *be* to identify things that aren't near us.

*That's my school and those are my friends.*

▶ 2.4

| | Things that are near | Things that aren't near |
|---|---|---|
| Singular | **This** is my wallet. | **That**'s my teacher. |
| Plural | **These** are my books. | **Those** are my classmates. |

**Look!** We can also use *this/that/these/those* + noun. *That book is new.*

1 Choose the correct words to complete the sentences.

1 *This* / *These* is my room.
2 Excuse me. Are *that* / *those* your glasses?
3 Look! Is *this* / *that* your phone over there?
4 Are *these* / *this* your keys?
5 Is *that* / *those* your pen, or is it my pen?
6 Are *these* / *this* your credit cards?

◀ Go back to page 15

## 2C Possessive adjectives, 's for possession

We use possessive adjectives before nouns to say that something belongs to someone.

*Joseph is my brother.*   *This is our house.*

We use the same possessive adjectives for singular and plural nouns.

*Is that your key?*   *Are those your keys?*

▶ 2.11 **Possessive adjectives**

| my | I'm French. **My** wife is Spanish. |
| your | Are **you** sad? **Your** boyfriend isn't here. |
| his | **He**'s a teacher. **His** students are young. |
| her | **She**'s an actor. **Her** house is big. |
| its | **It**'s a small restaurant. **Its** pizzas are good. |
| our | **We**'re late. **Our** boss isn't happy. |
| their | **They**'re tour guides. **Their** jobs are interesting. |

If we talk about possession with a name or a noun, we add *'s* to the name or noun.

*Is that the teacher's book?*   *Are you Rob's sister?*

1 Complete the sentences with the correct possessive adjectives.

1 Hello. _____ name's Kate.
2 We're from Lima. This is a photo of _____ house.
3 He's French. _____ name is Olivier.
4 They're British, but _____ parents are from Peru.
5 Hi, I'm Tom. What's _____ name?
6 This is Luisa and _____ husband, Sven.

2 Complete the sentences with *'s* for possession so they mean the same as the first sentences.

1 She's Olivia. Those are her sunglasses.
   Those are *Olivia's sunglasses* .
2 He's my son. That's his credit card.
   That's _____ .
3 This is my daughter. Her name is Ruby.
   My _____ .
4 She's our doctor. Her phone number is 665342.
   Our _____ .

◀ Go back to page 19

97

## GRAMMAR PRACTICE

### 3A Present simple (*I, you, we, they*)

We use the present simple to talk about facts and routines.

*I drink coffee for breakfast.*
*We eat a lot of fruit.*

We form negatives with *don't* (*do not*) + the infinitive of the verb.

*My parents don't like tea.*
*They don't eat meat.*

We form questions with *do* + subject + the infinitive of the verb.

*Do you like fish?*
*Do they have breakfast?*

| ▶ 3.3 | I / you / we / they |
|---|---|
| + | I **have** a big breakfast.<br>You **eat** a lot of fruit. |
| – | We **don't drink** coffee.<br>They **don't like** cheese. |
| ? | **Do** you **have** a big breakfast?<br>**Do** they **eat** fish? |
| Y/N | Yes, I **do**. / No, I **don't**.<br>Yes, they **do**. / No, they **don't**. |

**1** Complete the sentences with the correct form of the verbs in brackets.

1  I _____ pizza. (like)
2  We _____ eggs or cheese. (not eat)
3  They _____ lunch at home. (not have)
4  You _____ tea. (drink)
5  Our children _____ green vegetables. (not like)
6  My husband and I _____ a lot of fruit. (eat)
7  I _____ coffee at night. (not drink)
8  You _____ breakfast. (not have)

**2** Order the words to make questions. Then complete the short answers.

1  you / meat / eat / do
   _____ ? No, I _____ .
2  you / do / food / like / Indian
   _____ ? Yes, we _____ .
3  potatoes / they / like / do
   _____ ? Yes, they _____ .
4  drink / do / you and Anna / coffee
   _____ ? No, we _____ .

◀ Go back to page 25

### 3C Present simple (*he, she, it*)

For *he, she* and *it*, we often add *-s* to the infinitive to make the positive form.

*I drink tea for breakfast.* ⇒ *He drinks tea for breakfast.*

| Spelling rules for present simple verbs with *he, she, it* |
|---|
| We usually add *-s* to the infinitive.<br>*work* ⇒ *works* |
| When a verb ends in a consonant + *y*, we remove the *y* and then add *-ies*.<br>*study* ⇒ *studies* |
| When a verb ends in *ch*, *sh*, *s* or *x*, we add *-es*.<br>*watch* ⇒ *watches* |
| Some verbs are irregular.<br>*go* ⇒ *goes*   *do* ⇒ *does*   *have* ⇒ *has* |

We form negatives with *doesn't* (*does not*) + the infinitive of the verb.

*My sister doesn't speak English.*

We form questions with *does* + subject + the infinitive of the verb.

*Does our teacher work at the weekend?*

| ▶ 3.14 | he / she / it |
|---|---|
| + | Kevin **does** exercise in the morning.<br>She **lives** in Scotland. |
| – | He **doesn't want** a new car.<br>My house **doesn't have** a garden. |
| ? | **Does** he **live** in London?<br>**Does** Sandra **go** to the gym? |
| Y/N | Yes, he **does**. / No, he **doesn't**.<br>Yes, she **does**. / No, she **doesn't**. |

**1** Write the present simple *he, she, it* form of the verbs.

1  like   _____     5  go     _____
2  have   _____     6  try    _____
3  play   _____     7  drink  _____
4  eat    _____     8  wash   _____

**2** Rewrite the sentences. Use positive (+), negative (–) or question (?) forms.

1  My father makes good cakes.
   _____ (?)
2  Anna doesn't study at university.
   _____ (+)
3  Mark works on Tuesday.
   _____ (–)
4  Does she have two children?
   _____ (+)
5  Sam thinks about football all day.
   _____ (?)
6  My sister doesn't watch TV in the evening.
   _____ (+)

◀ Go back to page 29

# GRAMMAR PRACTICE

## 4A Adverbs of frequency

We use adverbs of frequency with the present simple to talk about routines.

*They always go to the gym on Friday.*
*I sometimes play football at the weekend.*

Adverbs of frequency come before most verbs, but we put adverbs of frequency after the verb *be*.

*I usually have lunch at work.*
*I'm always at home in the evening.* NOT *I always am at home in the evening.*

| ▶ 4.3 | Adverbs of frequency | |
|---|---|---|
| always | He **always** has a shower in the morning. | 100% |
| usually | Julia **usually** gets up early. | |
| often | You **often** get home after 9.00 p.m. | |
| sometimes | I'm **sometimes** late for class. | |
| never | My parents **never** drink coffee. | 0% |

**Look!** *never* has a negative meaning, but we use a positive form.
*My children never get up early.* NOT *My children don't never get up early.*

1 Order the words to make sentences.
1 brother / never / my / up / gets / early
   _____.
2 office / I / have / usually / lunch / at / the
   _____.
3 trains / late / always / the / night / at / are
   _____.
4 always / the / morning / a / have / I / in / shower
   _____.
5 dressed / I / get / usually / breakfast / before
   _____.
6 friendly / very / is / teacher / my / always
   _____.
7 never / we / dinner / before / have / 9.00 p.m.
   _____.
8 videos / watch / sometimes / in / we / class
   _____.

◀ Go back to page 33

## 4C Present simple: *wh-* questions

We ask questions with question words to ask for specific information.

A day / time of day – **When** does your brother go to the gym?
A time – **What time** does the class start?
A thing – **What** do you drink at work?
A person – **Who** do you work with?
A place – **Where** do you live?
A reason – **Why** do you get up early on Saturday?
A number – **How many** keys do you have?
An age – **How old** is Julian?
A manner – **How** do you get to work?

The word order in questions with most verbs is question word + *do/does* + subject + main verb + rest of question.

| ▶ 4.8 | Question word | do/does | Subject | Main verb | Rest of question |
|---|---|---|---|---|---|
| | What | do | you | have | for breakfast? |
| | When | does | she | see | her friends? |
| | Where | do | his parents | work? | |

With the verb *be*, the word order in questions is question word + *am/is/are* + subject + rest of question.

| ▶ 4.9 | Question word | am/is/are | Subject | Rest of question |
|---|---|---|---|---|
| | Why | am | I | cold? |
| | What time | is | | the bus? |
| | How | are | you | today? |

1 Complete the questions with the question words in the box.

| How many    What    What time |
| When    Where    Why |

1 _____ does your brother do?
   He's a taxi driver.
2 _____ do you usually play tennis?
   I usually play at the weekend.
3 _____ does your sister work?
   She works at the hospital.
4 _____ do you like your job?
   Because I meet a lot of people and it's interesting.
5 _____ does your English class start?
   At 7.30 p.m.
6 _____ cousins do you have?
   I have eight cousins.

2 Write questions.
1 What / you / want for dinner?
   _____
2 Why / he / cycle to work?
   _____
3 Who / be / your favourite actors?
   _____
4 How / they / know that man?
   _____
5 Where / your mum / go shopping?
   _____
6 What time / the lesson / finish?
   _____

◀ Go back to page 37

# GRAMMAR PRACTICE

## 5A *can* and *can't*

We use *can* and *can't* (*cannot*) to talk about ability.
*I can play the piano.   My grandmother can't drive.*
To make questions with *can*, we put *can* before the subject.
*Can you speak Portuguese?   What can he cook?*
We use the same form for all people and things.
*I/You/He/She/It/We/They can swim.*

| ▶ 5.3 | I / you / he / she / it / we / they |
|---|---|
| + | I **can speak** Italian. |
| − | You **can't play** the violin. |
| ? | **Can** he **cook** Chinese food? |
| Y/N | Yes, he **can**. / No, he **can't**. |

**Look!** We use *can/can't* with *well* to say we are good/bad at something.
*She can speak English well.*
*They can't swim well.*

1 Write positive (+) or negative (−) sentences with *can*.
   1 My sister / drive. (−)
      _____
   2 Dogs / swim. (+)
      _____
   3 Her son / use a computer. (−)
      _____
   4 My dad / cook well. (+)
      _____

2 Complete the questions. Use *can* and the verbs in brackets. Then write the short answers.
   1 A _____ Sarah _____ 10 km? (run)
      B Yes, _____ .
   2 A _____ you and Jo _____ salsa? (dance)
      B No, _____ .
   3 A _____ your son _____ Italian food? (cook)
      B Yes, _____ .
   4 A _____ you _____ well? (sing)
      B No, _____ .

◀ Go back to page 43

## 5C Object pronouns

The object of a sentence is the noun which comes after the verb.
*I like biscuits.* (*biscuits* are the object of the sentence)
*Ana calls her sister every week.* (*her sister* is the object of the sentence)
We use object pronouns instead of nouns when we know what the noun is.
*Emily is a really nice person. I like her.* (*her* = Emily)
*Fruit juice is good for you. I drink it for breakfast.* (*it* = fruit juice)

| ▶ 5.14 | Subject pronouns | Object pronouns | |
|---|---|---|---|
| | I | me | I'm here. Can you see **me**? |
| | you | you | You're friendly. I like **you**. |
| | he | him | Paul's a doctor. We work with **him**. |
| | she | her | Who is Karen? I don't know **her**. |
| | it | it | I love walking. Do you like **it**? |
| | we | us | We're at work. Call **us** if you have a problem. |
| | you | you | You and Ben are only 12 years old. Your parents look after **you**. |
| | they | them | I have three cats. I love **them**! |

**Look!** We always use object pronouns, not subject pronouns, after prepositions.
*Can you come with me?*
*Where's Paul? I want to talk to him.*

1 Replace the underlined words with object pronouns.

   1 I love <u>books</u>.   _____
   2 My sister has <u>the car</u>.   _____
   3 He doesn't like <u>Maria</u>.   _____
   4 They cook for <u>my wife and me</u>.   _____
   5 Give the book to <u>John</u>.   _____
   6 Can he help <u>you and Abdul</u>?   _____

2 Choose the correct words to complete the sentences.
   1 Ivan's a waiter. I see *he / him* at work.
   2 Lucy lives in France, but *she / her* isn't French.
   3 I hate cleaning. Why do I do *me / it*?
   4 Your children are quiet. Where are *they / them*?
   5 This bike is very fast. Do you want *it / them*?
   6 Can you look after my plant? *It / Her* needs water every day.

◀ Go back to page 47

100

# GRAMMAR PRACTICE

## 6A there is/are

We use *there's* (*there is*) + *a/an* with singular nouns to say that something exists.

*There's a beautiful park near my house.*
*There's an umbrella on the table.*

We use *there are* with plural nouns to say that something exists.

*There are five hotels in my city.*
*There are six people on the bus.*

We often use *some* in positive sentences with plural nouns. We use *any* in negative sentences and questions with plural nouns.

*There are some good cafés in the town centre.*
*There aren't any museums.*
*Are there any hotels near here?*

| ▶ 6.2 | Singular | Plural |
|---|---|---|
| + | There's a school. <br> There's an airport. | There are some schools. <br> There are two airports. |
| – | There isn't a cinema. | There aren't any cinemas. |
| ? | Is there a restaurant? | Are there any restaurants? |
| Y/N | Yes, there is. / <br> No, there isn't. | Yes, there are. / <br> No, there aren't. |

**1** Complete the sentences with the correct forms of *there is/are*.

1 _____ a great museum in town.
2 _____ a school near your house?
3 I'm sorry, but _____ a chemist near here.
4 _____ some cheap hotels near the train station.
5 _____ any parks, so children play in the street.
6 _____ any good restaurants at the shopping centre?

**2** Complete the sentences with *a/an*, *some* or *any*.

1 There aren't _____ supermarkets in this area.
2 There's _____ good hospital near here.
3 There are _____ police officers in the street.
4 There isn't _____ Italian restaurant in our village.
5 Are there _____ pens in your bag?
6 Is there _____ police station near here?

◀ Go back to page 51

## 6C Prepositions of place

We use prepositions of place to say where an object or person is.

*There's a table next to the bed.*    *Your keys are behind the sofa.*
*My brother is in the kitchen.*    *Simon is next to Amy.*

▶ 6.9 Prepositions of place

| on | The phone is **on** the table. |
| in | The phone is **in** the bag. |
| above | The shelves are **above** the table. |
| under | The bag is **under** the table. |

| next to | The chair is **next to** the table. |
| in front of | The table is **in front of** the chair. |
| between | The chair is **between** the window and the table. |
| behind | The lamp is **behind** the sofa. |

**1** Look at the picture. Write sentences saying where the things are with prepositions of place.

1 fridge / cooker
_____
2 shelves / bed
_____
3 cat / table
_____
4 laptop / desk
_____
5 window / sofa
_____
6 table / sofa
_____

◀ Go back to page 55

101

## GRAMMAR PRACTICE

## 7A Past simple: *be*

We use the past simple of the verb *be* to talk about situations in the past.

*Marilyn Monroe was an actor. She was American.*

The positive past simple forms of the verb *be* are *was* and *were*.

*I was in New York yesterday. The people were very friendly.*

The negative past simple forms of the verb *be* are *wasn't* (*was not*) and *weren't* (*were not*).

*I wasn't at home last night.*
*The Beatles weren't from Manchester.*

We form questions with *was/were* + subject.

*Was the teacher late for class?*
*Were you cold at work today?*

| ▶ 7.2 | I / he / she / it | you / we / they |
|---|---|---|
| + | I **was** happy. | They **were** singers. |
| – | It **wasn't** a good film. | We **weren't** at home yesterday. |
| ? | **Was** she at school? | **Were** they Mexican? |
| Y/N | Yes, she **was**. / No, she **wasn't**. | Yes, they **were**. / No, they **weren't**. |

**1** Choose the correct words to complete the sentences.

1 My father *was / were* an artist.
2 Enrique and Javier *wasn't / weren't* at work on Monday.
3 How *was / were* your holiday?
4 This book *wasn't / weren't* very interesting.
5 My grandparents *was / were* both musicians.
6 What *was / were* the answer to this question?
7 *Were / Was* you and your sister at home yesterday?
8 We *wasn't / weren't* happy with our exam results.

**2** Complete the conversations with the correct form of *was* or *were*.

1 A _____ you at home yesterday?
  B No, I _____ . I _____ at the hospital.
2 A _____ the film good?
  B Yes, it _____ . The actors _____ amazing.
3 A _____ your parents teachers?
  B No, they _____ . They _____ writers.
4 A _____ Akira Kurosawa a photographer?
  B No, he _____ . He _____ a film director.
5 A _____ you late for school today?
  B Yes, I _____ . I _____ 30 minutes late.
6 A _____ you and Nico at the same school?
  B Yes, we _____ , but we _____ in the same class.

◀ Go back to page 61

## 7C Past simple: regular verbs

We use the past simple to talk about completed actions in the past. We usually add *-ed* to the infinitive to form the past simple of regular verbs.

cook ⇒ cooked    *I cooked pasta yesterday.*

**Spelling rules for regular positive past simple *verbs***

We usually add **-ed** to the infinitive.
cook ⇒ cooked

When a verb ends in **-e**, we add **-d**.
dance ⇒ danced

When a verb ends in consonant + **y**, we change the **y** to **i** and then we add **-ed**.
study ⇒ studied

When a verb ends in vowel + consonant, we usually double the consonant and add **-ed**.
stop ⇒ stopped

We form the negative with *didn't* (*did not*) + infinitive.

*I didn't want coffee for breakfast.*    *My parents didn't like the food.*

We form questions with *did* + subject + infinitive.

*Did she play the piano yesterday?*    *Did your brother live in Canada?*

| ▶ 7.12 | I / you / he / she / it / we / they |
|---|---|
| + | He **worked** in London. |
| – | They **didn't live** in this house. |
| ? | **Did** you **study** Spanish at university? |
| Y/N | Yes, I **did**. / No, I **didn't**. |

**1** Rewrite the sentences and questions in the past simple.

1 My grandfather lives in this street.
_____
2 I cook paella for dinner.
_____
3 She doesn't cycle home.
_____
4 The train doesn't stop in Paris.
_____
5 Liam studies Science at university.
_____
6 Does she dance with her friends?
_____
7 Do they live in Ecuador?
_____
8 Elise doesn't want ice cream.
_____

◀ Go back to page 65

102

GRAMMAR PRACTICE

## 8A Past simple: irregular verbs

A lot of common verbs have an irregular past simple form (for a full list of irregular verbs see page 151).

take ⇨ took    I **took** a taxi to the airport.
go ⇨ went      We **went** to the park yesterday.
buy ⇨ bought   I **bought** a new bag.

Only the positive forms are irregular. We form the negative with *didn't* + infinitive.

*We didn't take the train.*
*They didn't go to the party.*
*My sister didn't buy coffee.*

We form questions with *did* + subject + infinitive.

*Did they take the train?*
*Did you go to the supermarket?*
*Did we buy any vegetables?*

| ▶ 8.2 | I / you / he / she / it / we / they |
|---|---|
| + | He **went** to university in Edinburgh. |
| − | She **didn't have** breakfast yesterday. |
| ? | **Did** you **see** Carly at the party? |
| Y/N | Yes, I **did**. / No, I **didn't**. |

1 Complete the sentences with the past simple form of the verbs in brackets.
   1 They _____ to work by car. (go)
   2 She _____ to Hong Kong. (fly)
   3 I _____ on the 11.30 bus to Newcastle. (get)
   4 Paula _____ her daughter a lot of stories. (tell)
   5 Richard _____ coffee and toast for breakfast. (have)
   6 Clarissa _____ 'Hi'. (say)
   7 I _____ pasta for dinner. (make)
   8 My mum _____ to work yesterday. (drive)

2 Complete the questions and answers with the correct form of the verbs in brackets.
   1 A What time _____ her train _____ ? (leave)
     B It _____ at 8.00 p.m.
   2 A _____ you _____ a dress to the party? (wear)
     B No, I _____ a dress. I _____ jeans.
   3 A _____ he _____ a bus to the station? (take)
     B No, he _____ a bus. He _____ the underground.
   4 A _____ you _____ well last night? (sleep)
     B No, I _____ at all!
   5 A _____ you _____ a big lunch? (have)
     B No, I _____ . I _____ a sandwich.
   6 A _____ you _____ to your dad yesterday? (speak)
     B No, but I _____ to my mum.

◀ Go back to page 69

## 8C there was/were

We use *there was/were* and *a/an* with singular nouns to say that something existed in the past.

*There was a big school here 50 years ago.*
*There was an egg in the fridge yesterday.*

We use *there were* with plural nouns to say that something existed in the past.

*There were lots of fields here in the past.*
*There were two books on my desk.*

We often use *some* in positive sentences with plural nouns. We use *any* in negative sentences and questions.

*There were some people in the shop.*
*There weren't any children.*
*Were there any cakes in the supermarket?*

| ▶ 8.9 | Singular | Plural |
|---|---|---|
| + | **There was** a road. **There was** an old house. | **There were** two shops. **There were some** trees. |
| − | **There wasn't** a supermarket. | **There weren't any** restaurants. |
| ? | **Was there** a school? | **Were there any** tall buildings? |
| Y/N | Yes, **there was**. / No, **there wasn't**. | Yes, **there were**. / No, **there weren't**. |

1 Look at the picture of Fairfield 100 years ago. Complete the sentences with the correct form of *there was/were* and *a/an* or *some/any*.

1 _____ supermarket, but _____ shops.
2 _____ cars in the village, but _____ bikes.
3 _____ cinema, but _____ nightclub.
4 _____ old tree and _____ flowers.

◀ Go back to page 73

103

# GRAMMAR PRACTICE

## 9A Present continuous

We use the present continuous to talk about actions that are happening now. We often use time expressions like *at the moment* and *now* with the present continuous.

*I'm wearing my new jeans today.*
*We aren't working at the moment.*
*What are you doing now?*

We form the present continuous with the verb *be* + the *-ing* form of the main verb.

### Spelling rules for the *-ing* form

We usually add *-ing* to the infinitive of the verb.
cook ⇨ cooking   watch ⇨ watching

When the verb ends in a consonant + **e**, we usually remove the **e** and then add *-ing*.
take ⇨ taking   dance ⇨ dancing

When the verb ends in a consonant + a vowel + a consonant, we double the consonant and then add *-ing*.
begin ⇨ beginning   get ⇨ getting

| ▶ 9.3 | I | he / she / it | you / we / they |
|---|---|---|---|
| + | I'm listening to music. | He's reading a book. | You're singing. |
| – | I'm not watching TV. | She isn't working. | We aren't stopping here. |
| ? | Am I sleeping? | Is he studying? | Are they going? |
| Y/N | Yes, I am. / No, I'm not. | Yes, he is. / No, he isn't. | Yes, they are. / No, they aren't. |

1 Write the *-ing* form of the verbs.
   1 buy _____   6 look _____
   2 drive _____   7 make _____
   3 sit _____   8 stop _____
   4 go _____   9 swim _____
   5 leave _____   10 watch _____

2 Write positive (+) sentences, negative (–) sentences or questions (?) in the present continuous.
   1 George / listen to / music / now (+)
   _____
   2 you / wear / a new coat (?)
   _____
   3 she / listen to / me (–)
   _____
   4 they / do / their homework (–)
   _____
   5 we / have dinner / at the moment (+)
   _____
   6 it / rain / today (?)
   _____

◀ Go back to page 79

## 9C *How often* + expressions of frequency

We use *How often ... ?* + the present simple or the verb *be* to ask about frequency.

*How often do you go shopping?*
*How often does Tim go to London?*
*How often are you late for class?*

We can answer the question *How often ...?* with expressions of frequency.

*How often are your English classes?*
*I have a class once or twice a week.* (*once* = one time, *twice* = two times)

| ▶ 9.13 | Expressions of frequency |
|---|---|
| every day/week/month/year | I go to the gym **every day**. |
| once a day/week/month/year | John has a holiday **once a year**. |
| twice a day/week/month/year | Ali has a coffee with his friends **twice a week**. |
| three/four times a day/week/month/year | They play football **three or four times a month**. |

**Look!** We can also answer questions with *How often ...?* with adverbs of frequency (*always, usually, often, sometimes, never*).
*How often do you walk to work?*
*I never walk to work. I usually get the bus.*

1 Complete the questions and answers. Use the words in brackets.

   1 How often _____ your bike? (you / ride)
     I _____ my bike _____ day.
   2 How often _____ in your city? (it / snow)
     It only _____ once _____ year.
   3 How often _____ his grandparents? (Luis / see)
     He _____ his grandparents three _____ a month.
   4 How often _____ tennis? (you / play)
     We _____ tennis _____ weekend.
   5 How often _____ their friends? (they / meet)
     They _____ their friends twice _____ week.

◀ Go back to page 83

# GRAMMAR PRACTICE

## 10A Present continuous for future plans

We use the present continuous to talk about plans and arrangements in the future (for spelling rules of -ing forms see page 104).

*I'm going to the dentist next week.*

| ▶ 10.3 | I | he / she / it | you / we / they |
|---|---|---|---|
| + | I'm **meeting** friends tonight. | She's **taking** the bus tomorrow. | You're **working** next Tuesday. |
| − | I'm **not going** to school tomorrow. | He **isn't watching** a film tonight. | We **aren't playing** tennis later. |
| ? | **Am** I **working** this weekend? | **Is** she **staying** at home tonight? | **Are** they **going** to the gym? |
| Y/N | Yes, I **am**. / No, I'm **not**. | Yes, he **is**. / No, he **isn't**. | Yes, they **are**. / No, they **aren't**. |

We often use a future time expression to talk about future plans and arrangements. Time expressions usually go at the end of the sentence.

| ▶ 10.4 | Future time expressions |
|---|---|
| this morning/afternoon/evening | We're taking the train **this afternoon**. |
| tonight | What are you having for dinner **tonight**? |
| tomorrow | Sven isn't coming to the party **tomorrow**. |
| next week/month/year | We're going on holiday **next week**. |
| later | Are you meeting Jorge **later**? |

1 Complete the sentences and questions with the present continuous form of the verbs in the box.

| take | not visit | meet |
| not come | stay | watch |

1 We _____ our friends for dinner later.
2 _____ you _____ the football match tonight?
3 They _____ the 7.30 train to Edinburgh tomorrow.
4 He _____ with some friends in Lima at the weekend.
5 Maria is ill. She _____ to the concert this evening.
6 We _____ the museum next week. It's closed.

2 Write sentences and questions in the present continuous.

1 I / meet / my friends this weekend
_____ .
2 My brother / not visit / us this month
_____ .
3 They / not go / on holiday this summer
_____ .
4 What / you / cook / for dinner on Saturday
_____ ?

◀ Go back to page 87

## 10C Question review

Questions can be *yes/no* questions or they can ask for specific information with a question word (*where, when, who,* etc.).

*Do you live in Japan? Yes, I do./No, I don't.*
*Where are you from? I'm from Turkey.*

For most verbs, the word order in questions is: (question word +) auxiliary verb + subject + main verb + rest of question.

| ▶ 10.12 | (Question word) | Auxiliary verb | Subject | Main verb | Rest of question |
|---|---|---|---|---|---|
| **Present simple** | What | Does do | Chris you | speak have | English? for breakfast? |
| **Past simple** | When | Did did | Lucy you | call arrive | you yesterday? at the airport? |
| **Present continuous** | Where | Is are | it they | snowing going | now? next week? |

For the verbs *be* and *can*, the word order in questions is: (question word +) verb + subject + rest of question.

| ▶ 10.13 | (Question word) | Verb | Subject | Rest of question |
|---|---|---|---|---|
| ***be*** (present simple) | Where | Is are | Julia you | here? from? |
| ***be*** (past simple) | Who | Were was | you Philip | late for work? with? |
| ***can*** | What sports | Can can | you they | ride a motorbike? do? |

1 Order the words to make questions.

1 rock climbing / does / go / how often / he
_____ ?
2 you / what / for / lunch / are / having
_____ ?
3 homework / when / she / did / do / her
_____ ?
4 can / instrument / you / play / an
_____ ?
5 you / crying / why / are
_____ ?
6 did / where / he / on / go / holiday
_____ ?
7 they / were / home / night / last / at
_____ ?
8 what / is / she / time / leaving
_____ ?

◀ Go back to page 91

# VOCABULARY PRACTICE

## Hello Classroom language

1 ▶ 1.7 Listen and repeat.

1 Open your books.

2 Close your books.

3 Go to page 5.

4 Look at the picture.

5 Listen and repeat.

6 Work in pairs.

7 Excuse me, what does 'nice' mean?

8 Sorry, I don't understand.

9 How do you say 'bom dia' in English?

10 Can you repeat that, please?

11 How do you spell that?

12 Sorry I'm late.

2 Complete the conversation with the words in the box.

| go  open  listen  ~~late~~  look  spell  work  close  mean  repeat |
|---|

**Norio** Hello. Sorry I'm ¹ _late_ .
**Teacher** Hello. Are you Norio?
**Norio** Yes, I am.
**Teacher** I'm your teacher. My name's Helen.
**Norio** Hi.
**Teacher** ² _____ your book and go to page 6, please.
**Norio** Sorry, can you ³ _____ that?
**Teacher** Yes. ⁴ _____ to page 6 in your book.
**Norio** OK.
**Teacher** ⁵ _____ at the picture of a family.

**Norio** Excuse me, what does 'family' ⁶ _____ ?
**Teacher** Your mother, father, brothers, sisters …
**Norio** I understand. How do you ⁷ _____ 'family'?
**Teacher** F-A-M-I-L-Y.
**Norio** Thank you.
**Teacher** ⁸ _____ and repeat – 'family'.
**Norio** Family.
**Teacher** Very good. Now, ⁹ _____ your books and ¹⁰ _____ in pairs …

106  ◀ Go back to page 5

VOCABULARY PRACTICE

## 1A Countries and nationalities

1  ▶ 1.12 Listen and repeat.

1 Argentina
Argentinian

2 Brazil
Brazilian

3 Canada
Canadian

4 Chile
Chilean

5 China
Chinese

6 France
French

7 Germany
German

8 India
Indian

9 Italy
Italian

10 Japan
Japanese

11 Mexico
Mexican

12 Peru
Peruvian

13 Poland
Polish

14 Russia
Russian

15 Spain
Spanish

16 Turkey
Turkish

17 the UK
British

18 the USA
American

2  Look at the pictures. Complete the sentences with the correct country or nationality.

1 Lionel Messi is _____ .

2 Paris is in _____ .

3 A kimono comes from _____ .

4 Pasta is _____ food.

5 A panda is an animal from _____ .

6 Washington D.C. is the capital of _____ .

7 Machu Picchu is in _____ .

8 These are _____ dolls.

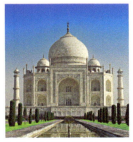
9 The Taj Mahal is in _____ .

10 Warsaw is a _____ city.

◀ Go back to page 6

VOCABULARY PRACTICE

## 1B Jobs

1 ▶ 1.19 Listen and repeat.

1 an actor

2 a chef

3 a doctor

4 an engineer

5 an IT worker

6 an office worker

7 a police officer

8 a receptionist

9 a shop assistant

10 a singer

11 a student

12 a taxi driver

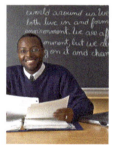
13 a teacher

14 a tour guide

15 a TV presenter

16 a waiter/a waitress

**Look!** We use *an* with jobs that begin with vowels (*a, e, i, o, u*) and *a* with jobs that begin with consonants (*b, c, d, f,* etc.).
I'm **a** teacher.
Are you **an** office worker?

2 Match the jobs in the box with objects 1–8. Use *a* or *an*.

| waiter   shop assistant   engineer   singer   receptionist   doctor   chef   actor |

1 _____

2 _____

3 _____

4 _____

5 _____

6 _____

7 _____

8 _____

108

◀ Go back to page 8

VOCABULARY PRACTICE

## 1C Adjectives (1)

1 ▶ 1.32 Listen and repeat.

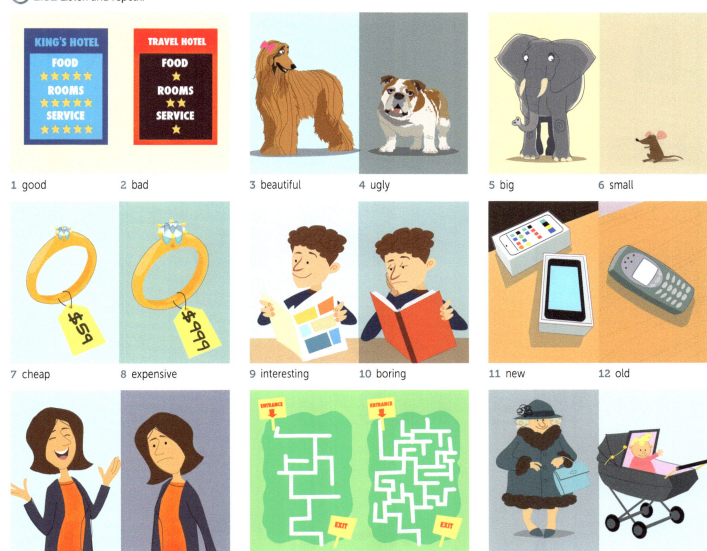

1 good   2 bad   3 beautiful   4 ugly   5 big   6 small
7 cheap   8 expensive   9 interesting   10 boring   11 new   12 old
13 happy   14 sad   15 easy   16 difficult   17 old   18 young

2 Choose the correct words to complete the conversations.

**A** This phone is ¹*cheap / boring*.
It's only £50.
**B** Yes, but it isn't ²*difficult / good*.
Look at this phone.
**A** It's £695! It's very ³*expensive / new*.

**A** How ⁶*good / old* is Michael?
**B** He's ⁷*new / young*. He's three years old today!
**A** He's very ⁸*happy / sad*.

**A** Hi, Sara. Do you understand Italian?
**B** Yes. I'm Spanish, but Italian is ⁴*big / easy* for me.
**A** Oh, that's ⁵*interesting / ugly*.

**A** Wow – this painting is ⁹*beautiful / difficult*!
**B** Yes, but it's very ¹⁰*bad / small*.
**A** My house is small, too!

◀ Go back to page 11

109

## VOCABULARY PRACTICE

### 2A Personal objects

1 ▶ 2.2 Listen and repeat.

1 a bag  2 a book  3 a camera  4 a credit card  5 glasses

6 keys  7 a mobile phone  8 a pen  9 a pencil  10 a purse

11 sunglasses  12 a tablet  13 an umbrella  14 a wallet  15 a watch

2 Write the objects you can see in the pictures.

1 _____  4 _____
2 _____  5 _____
3 _____  6 _____

◀ Go back to page 14

### 2B Colours

1 ▶ 2.8 Listen and repeat.

1 black  2 blue  3 brown  4 gold  5 green

6 grey  7 orange  8 pink  9 purple

10 red  11 silver  12 white  13 yellow

2 Write the colours.

1 red + blue = _____     4 black + white = _____
2 red + white = _____    5 red + yellow = _____
3 blue + yellow = _____  6 red + blue + yellow = _____

◀ Go back to page 16

110

**VOCABULARY PRACTICE**

## 1C  Numbers 0–100

1 ▶ 1.26 Listen and repeat.

| 0 zero/oh | 5 five | 10 ten | 15 fifteen | 20 twenty | 50 fifty | 100 a hundred/ |
|---|---|---|---|---|---|---|
| 1 one | 6 six | 11 eleven | 16 sixteen | 21 twenty-one | 60 sixty | one hundred |
| 2 two | 7 seven | 12 twelve | 17 seventeen | 22 twenty-two | 70 seventy | |
| 3 three | 8 eight | 13 thirteen | 18 eighteen | 30 thirty | 80 eighty | |
| 4 four | 9 nine | 14 fourteen | 19 nineteen | 40 forty | 90 ninety | |

2 Write the numbers as words or digits.

1 34 _____    3 63 _____    5 88 _____    7 29 _____    9 12 _____
2 ____ seventy-two    4 ____ ninety-one    6 ____ fifty-seven    8 ____ forty-four    10 ____ a hundred

◀ Go back to page 10

## 2C  Family and friends

1 ▶ 2.10 Listen and repeat.

1 grandfather    2 grandmother
3 grandparents

4 mother    5 father    7 son    8 daughter
6 parents    9 children

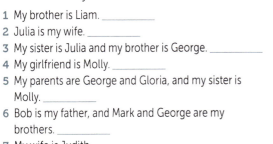
10 husband    11 wife

12 sister    13 brother

14 boyfriend    15 girlfriend

2 Look at the family tree. Read the sentences and write the names.

1 My brother is Liam. _____
2 Julia is my wife. _____
3 My sister is Julia and my brother is George. _____
4 My girlfriend is Molly. _____
5 My parents are George and Gloria, and my sister is Molly. _____
6 Bob is my father, and Mark and George are my brothers. _____
7 My wife is Judith. _____
8 My husband's brother is Mark. _____
9 Our children are Julia, Mark and George. _____ and _____
10 Our parents are Judith and Bob. _____ , _____ and _____

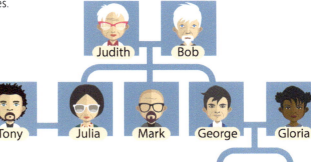

◀ Go back to page 18

VOCABULARY PRACTICE

## 3A Food and drink

1 ▶ 3.2 Listen and repeat.
Food

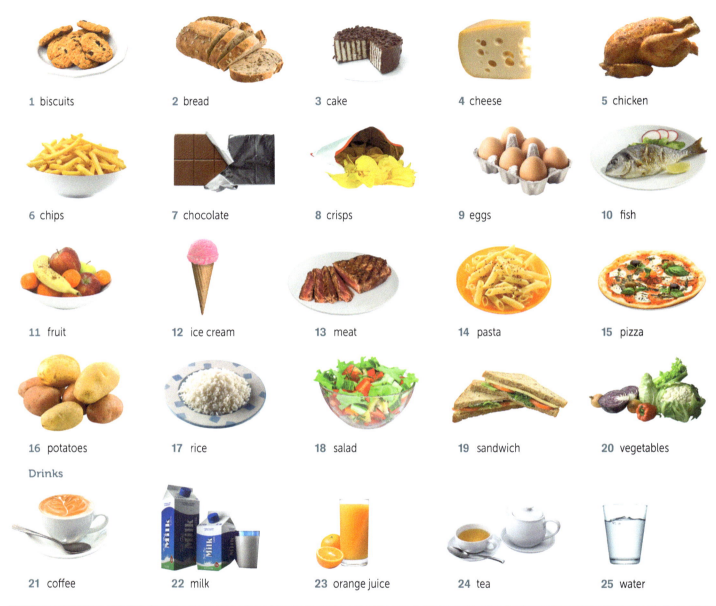

1 biscuits
2 bread
3 cake
4 cheese
5 chicken
6 chips
7 chocolate
8 crisps
9 eggs
10 fish
11 fruit
12 ice cream
13 meat
14 pasta
15 pizza
16 potatoes
17 rice
18 salad
19 sandwich
20 vegetables

Drinks

21 coffee
22 milk
23 orange juice
24 tea
25 water

**Look!** If we want to talk about the food and drink that we eat and drink at breakfast, lunch and dinner, we can use the verb *have*.
What do you **have** for breakfast/lunch/dinner?
I **have** coffee for breakfast. I **have** a sandwich for lunch. I **have** fish for dinner.

have breakfast — have lunch — have dinner

2 Choose the correct words to complete the sentences.
  1 Ice cream has *milk / cheese* in it.
  2 Potatoes are *fruit / vegetables*.
  3 Cake, biscuits and *chocolate / salad* are bad for you.
  4 Crisps and chips come from *potatoes / pasta*.
  5 British people have *rice / milk* in their tea.
  6 Spaghetti is a type of *bread / pasta*.
  7 I have *breakfast / lunch* at 8.00 a.m.
  8 Vegetarians don't eat *meat / salad*.
  9 I drink *orange juice / fish* in the morning.
  10 I have *chocolate / meat* and vegetables for dinner.

◀ Go back to page 24

# VOCABULARY PRACTICE

## 3C Common verbs (1)

1 ▶ 3.12 Listen and repeat.

1 **change** money

2 **do** exercise

3 **go** to school

4 **have** two children

5 **know** the answer

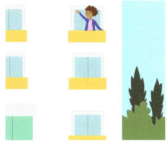
6 **live** in a flat

7 **make** coffee

8 **say** 'goodbye'

9 **study** German

10 **think** (about ...)

11 **use** a tablet

12 **want** a drink

13 **watch** a film

14 **work** in an office

> **Look!** We use *make* for food and drink:
> *They make very good cakes.*
>
> We use *do* for activities:
> *We do exercise in the morning.*
>
> We use *think* for thoughts and opinions:
> *I think about work.* (thought)
> *We think it's a good idea.* (opinion)

2 Choose the correct words to complete the sentences.

1 After work, I *know / go / use* to the gym.
2 I *study / say / live* English and Spanish at university.
3 My daughter and I *make / do / work* cakes at the weekend.
4 I *think / know / work* in a restaurant – I'm a waitress!
5 A Do you like that book?
   B No, I *think / watch / use* it's boring.
6 My boyfriend and I *watch / say / live* TV in the evening.
7 Do you *make / do / go* exercise at the weekend?
8 Do they *use / know / live* in a big house?
9 I *study / live / say* 'good morning' to people at work.
10 My mobile phone is old. I *watch / want / work* a new one.
11 A What's the capital of China?
    B I don't *go / use / know*.
12 My children *use / say / make* the internet a lot.

◀ Go back to page 28

# VOCABULARY PRACTICE

## 4A Daily routine verbs

1  ▶ 4.2 Listen and repeat.

1 get up

2 have a shower

3 get dressed

4 leave home

5 start work

6 go shopping

7 listen to the radio

8 do housework / homework

9 finish work

10 get home

11 go to bed

12 read a book

2  Complete the text with the correct form of the verbs in the box.

| do (x2)   get (x3)   go (x2)   leave   finish   listen   start   have |
|---|

I'm Miranda and this is my typical day. I [1]_____ up at 7.00 in the morning and [2]_____ a shower. Then I have breakfast with my son, Leon. He [3]_____ dressed and then we [4]_____ home at about 8.30 a.m. Leon goes to school and I'm an office worker. I [5]_____ work at 9.00 a.m.
I [6]_____ work at 3.00 p.m. and go to Leon's school. We [7]_____ shopping and [8]_____ home at about 4.00 in the afternoon. In the evening, Leon [9]_____ his homework and I make dinner. After dinner, Leon [10]_____ to bed at 8.00 p.m. and I [11]_____ the housework and [12]_____ to the radio. I go to bed at 11.00 p.m. … and the next day, we do it all again!

114                                                        ◀ Go back to page 32

**VOCABULARY PRACTICE**

## 4B Transport

**1** ▶ 4.6 Listen and repeat.

1 by bike

2 by boat

3 by bus

4 by car

5 by ferry

6 by lorry

7 by motorbike

8 by plane

9 by taxi

10 by train

11 on foot

12 on the subway/underground/metro

**Look!** Different cities have different names for their underground trains.
*In New York, I go on the **subway**.    In London, I go on the **underground**.    In Sydney, I go on the **metro**.*

**2** Match the types of transport in the box with the pictures.

| lorry   taxi   underground   ferry   train   plane   boat   motorbike |
|---|

**3** Complete the sentences with the correct types of transport and *by* or *on*.

1 I go _____ 🚲 to the train station. Then I go _____ 🚌 to the city. After that, I go _____ 🚶 to the office.

2 Lucia goes _____ 🚕 to the airport. Then she goes _____ ✈ to New York. After that, she goes _____ 🚇 to the city centre.

3 We go _____ 🚗 to Dover, but my brother goes _____ 🏍. Then we all go _____ 🚢 to France.

◀ Go back to page 34

VOCABULARY PRACTICE

## 3B Days and times of day

1 ▶ 3.7 Listen and repeat.

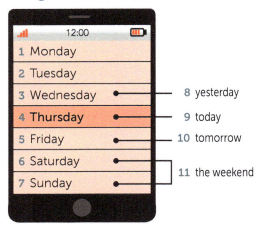
1 Monday
2 Tuesday
3 Wednesday
4 Thursday
5 Friday
6 Saturday
7 Sunday
8 yesterday
9 today
10 tomorrow
11 the weekend

12 morning   13 afternoon

14 evening   15 night

**Look!** We use the preposition *on* with days of the week, *in* with *the morning*, *the afternoon* and *the evening* and *at* with *the weekend* and *night*.
*I eat fish **on** Friday.*
*I have breakfast **in** the morning.*
*I drink milk **at** night.*

We also say *on* + day and time of day:
*on Wednesday morning, on Friday afternoon*, etc.

2 Choose the correct words to complete the sentences and questions.

1 My birthday is *on / in / at* Sunday.
2 I have dinner *on / in / at* the evening.
3 We don't drink coffee at *afternoon / evening / night*.
4 I have lunch with Emma on *the weekend / Friday / the morning*.
5 Is your English lesson *on / in / at* Thursday evening?
6 They have breakfast at 9.00 in *the weekend / Wednesday / the morning*.
7 Is Marcus on holiday *on / in / at* Thursday?
8 They aren't at university *on / in / at* Wednesday afternoon.
9 What do you have for lunch at *the afternoon / the weekend / Monday*?
10 On Sunday, I have chicken for lunch *on / in / at* the afternoon.

◀ Go back to page 26

## 4C Adjectives (2)

1 ▶ 4.7 Listen and repeat.

1 cold   2 hot   3 clean   4 dirty   5 fast   6 slow   7 friendly   8 unfriendly

9 nice   10 horrible   11 large   12 small   13 long   14 short   15 noisy   16 quiet

2 Complete the text with the adjectives in the box.

| noisy   cold   quiet   hot   short   friendly   dirty   large |

Hi, I'm Matt. I'm a student in Edinburgh, Scotland. I always get up at 8.30 and I have a ¹_____ tea for breakfast. Then I go to the university on foot. It's sometimes ²_____ in the mornings, but that's OK – it's only a ³_____ walk.

I live in a ⁴_____ house with eight students. They're really ⁵_____ . We always make dinner together, and sometimes there are a lot of ⁶_____ dishes when we finish! My housemates play music and the house is sometimes ⁷_____ , so I usually work in the library – it's always ⁸_____ there.

116   ◀ Go back to page 36

**VOCABULARY PRACTICE**

## 5A Common verbs (2)

1 ▶ 5.1 Listen and repeat.

1 **arrive** at the airport
2 **call** my mother
3 **cook** fish

4 **dance** salsa
5 **drive** a car
6 **give** a present

7 **help** my grandmother

8 **look after** my daughter

9 **meet** friends

10 **play** football

11 **play** the piano

12 **sing**

13 **speak** Italian
14 **swim** in the sea

15 **travel** by bus

2 Complete the sentences with the correct form of the verbs in the box.

| cook  meet  give  arrive  help  drive  speak  play (x2)  travel  sing  call  look after |
|---|

1 Simon _____ Portuguese.
2 I _____ dinner at the weekend.
3 Sharon often _____ basketball.
4 My father _____ a bus.
5 I always _____ my son with his homework.
6 We usually _____ by train.
7 I sometimes _____ my friend's dog.
8 We _____ in Lima at 9.15 a.m.
9 I always _____ Lucy for a coffee after work.
10 You never _____ me flowers.
11 Jo likes music. She _____ and _____ the guitar.
12 My parents live in India, so I _____ them on Skype.

◀ Go back to page 42

117

# VOCABULARY PRACTICE

## 5B Electronic devices

**1** ▶ 5.8 Listen and repeat.

1 desktop computer

2 DVD player

3 DVR (digital video recorder)

4 earphones

5 headphones

6 laptop

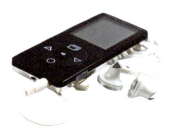

7 MP3 player

8 radio

9 remote control

10 Sat Nav

11 smartphone

12 TV (television)

**2** ~~Cross out~~ the word which is incorrect in each sentence.

1 **A** Listen to this song on my phone – it's great!
   **B** One moment – I need some *earphones / remote control / headphones*.
2 **A** Can I check my emails?
   **B** Yes. You can use my *radio / laptop / smartphone*.
3 **A** My friend lives on Bridge Street, but I don't know where that is.
   **B** It's OK. I have *a smartphone / a Sat Nav / an MP3 player*. We can use that.
4 **A** Do you want to watch a film tonight?
   **B** We can't, sorry. I don't have a *remote control / TV / DVD player*.
5 **A** I work at home. I have a *laptop / TV / desktop computer* and that's all I need.
   **B** At home? What a nice job!
6 **A** It's quiet. Why don't we listen to some music?
   **B** OK … where is the *radio / Sat Nav / MP3 player*?
7 **A** The news is on at 12.00.
   **B** OK, the *DVD player / TV / radio* is over there.
8 **A** Do you have a TV?
   **B** No, I don't. I watch TV shows on my *laptop / radio / smartphone*.

◀ Go back to page 44

# VOCABULARY PRACTICE

## 5C Activities

1 ▶ 5.13 Listen and repeat.

1 cleaning

2 cooking

3 cycling

4 dancing

5 going out

6 listening to music

7 meeting friends

8 reading

9 running

10 shopping

11 sleeping

12 swimming

13 walking

14 watching TV/films

**Look!** We can use activities that end in *-ing* or nouns with the verbs *like*, *love* and *hate*.
*I like shopping. I love clothes!*
*I don't like cycling. I hate bikes.*

2 Match the activities in the box with pictures 1–8.

| swimming   reading   running   cooking   cycling   cleaning   shopping   sleeping |

1 _____

2 _____

3 _____

4 _____

5 _____

6 _____

7 _____

8 _____

◀ Go back to page 46

# VOCABULARY PRACTICE

## 6A Places in a town

1 ▶ 6.1 Listen and repeat.

1 bank

2 bus stop

3 café

4 cinema

5 hospital

6 hotel

7 museum

8 nightclub

9 park

10 police station

11 post office

12 restaurant

13 school

14 shopping centre

15 supermarket

16 train station

### Look!

a village

a town

a city

A village is small.
A town is medium-sized.
A city is big.

2 Match the places in the box with jobs 1–5.

| hospital   police station   school |
| restaurant   shopping centre |

1 waiter _____
2 police officer _____
3 shop assistant _____
4 teacher _____
5 doctor _____

3 Complete the sentences with the places in the box.

| bank   nightclub   train station   park   post office |
| supermarket   bus stop   café   cinema   museum |

1 You can send a letter at a _____ .
2 You can get a train at a _____ .
3 You wait for a bus at a _____ .
4 You drink tea or coffee at a _____ .
5 You can dance at a _____ .
6 You watch a film at a _____ .
7 You see interesting things at a _____ .
8 You get money at a _____ .
9 You walk, play games or relax in a _____ .
10 You can buy food and drink at a _____ .

◀ Go back to page 50

VOCABULARY PRACTICE

## 6B Parts of the body

1 ▶ 6.7 Listen and repeat.

**Look!** The plural of *tooth* is *teeth*. The plural of *foot* is *feet*.

1 hair
2 head
3 ear
4 face
5 eye
6 nose
7 tooth (teeth)
8 mouth
9 body
10 arm
11 hand
12 leg
13 knee
14 foot (feet)

2 Put the parts of the body in the box in the correct columns.

| arms   body   ears   face   feet   hands   head   knees   legs   mouth   nose   teeth |

| I have one … | I have two … | I have more than two … |
|---|---|---|
| | | |

◀ Go back to page 52

121

## VOCABULARY PRACTICE

## 6C Rooms and furniture

1 ▶ 6.8 Listen and repeat.

2 Complete the sentences with the rooms and furniture in the box.

| fridge bath table sofa desk window bedroom cooker wardrobe shelves |

1 Let's have dinner in the living room. We can sit on the _____ and watch a film.
2 Shona has a big white _____ for all her clothes.
3 My favourite room is the _____ . I sleep there and it's very quiet.
4 After they make dinner, the _____ is very hot.
5 My bathroom is small, so I have a shower, but I don't have a _____ .
6 Ken needs a lot of _____ because he has hundreds of books!
7 It's hot in here. Can you open the _____ ?
8 Please put the milk and orange juice in the _____ .
9 I have a _____ in my bedroom where I do homework and use my laptop.
10 Dinner is ready. The food is on the _____ !

◀ Go back to page 54

# VOCABULARY PRACTICE

## 7A Celebrities

1 ▶ 7.1 Listen and repeat.

 1 artist
 2 athlete
 3 dancer
 4 DJ
 5 fashion model
 6 film director
 7 footballer
 8 journalist
 9 king
 10 musician
 11 photographer
 12 politician
 13 queen
 14 racing driver
 15 tennis player
 16 writer

2 Look at the pictures and complete the sentences with the words in the box.

| fashion model   writer   queen   musician   tennis player   dancer   king   film director   artist   footballer   politician   athlete |
|---|

 1 Shelly-Ann Fraser-Pryce is a Jamaican _____.
 2 Gisele Bündchen is a Brazilian _____.
 3 Emmanuel Macron is a French _____.
 4 Isabel Allende is a Chilean _____.
 5 Thomas Müller is a German _____.
 6 Margrethe II is the _____ of Denmark.
 7 Salvador Dalí was a Spanish _____.
 8 Beyoncé is an American _____.
 9 Sofia Coppola is an American _____.
 10 Venus Williams is an American _____.
 11 Felipe VI is the _____ of Spain.
 12 Rudolf Nureyev was a Russian _____.

◀ Go back to page 60

**VOCABULARY PRACTICE**

## 7B Months and ordinals

1 ▶ 7.5 Listen and repeat.

| 1 January | 2 February | 3 March | 4 April |
|---|---|---|---|
| 5 May | 6 June | 7 July | 8 August |
| 9 September | 10 October | 11 November | 12 December |

2 ▶ 7.6 Listen and repeat.

| 1st | first | 7th | seventh | 13th | thirteenth | 19th | nineteenth |
|---|---|---|---|---|---|---|---|
| 2nd | second | 8th | eighth | 14th | fourteenth | 20th | twentieth |
| 3rd | third | 9th | ninth | 15th | fifteenth | 21st | twenty-first |
| 4th | fourth | 10th | tenth | 16th | sixteenth | 22nd | twenty-second |
| 5th | fifth | 11th | eleventh | 17th | seventeenth | 30th | thirtieth |
| 6th | sixth | 12th | twelfth | 18th | eighteenth | 31st | thirty-first |

**Look!** In British English the ordinal comes before the month.
*2 February = the second of February*
*16 June = the sixteenth of June*
But in American English, the ordinal comes after the month.
*February 2 = February second*
*June 16 = June sixteenth*

3 Look at the dates in brackets and complete the sentences with the words.
   1 St Valentine's Day is the _____ of _____ . (14/02)
   2 Independence Day in the USA is the _____ of _____ . (04/07)
   3 New Year's Day is the _____ of _____ . (01/01)
   4 Halloween is the _____ of _____ . (31/10)
   5 My birthday is the _____ of _____ . (25/07)
   6 Mother's Day in the UK this year is the _____ of _____ . (11/03)

◀ Go back to page 62

## 7C Time expressions

1 ▶ 7.14 Listen and repeat.
   1 last         last night, last week, last year
   2 ago          two days ago, three weeks ago, four years ago
   3 yesterday    yesterday morning, yesterday afternoon, yesterday evening
   4 times        at 9.00, at 11.30, at midnight
   5 days         on Monday, on Tuesday, at the weekend
   6 dates        on 1 January, on 24 April, on 11 December
   7 years        in 1985, in 2001, in 2018
   8 decades      in the 1960s, in the 1990s, in the 2010s

**Look!** We say *yesterday morning/afternoon/evening*, but **last** night, NOT ~~yesterday~~ night.

2 Complete the sentences with the words in the box.

   on (x2)   in   ago   last (x2)   yesterday   at

   1 I studied English _____ morning. Then I watched TV.
   2 We enjoyed your party _____ night. It was great!
   3 Slavska meets her friends _____ 6.30 after work.
   4 I lived in Madrid _____ the 1980s. It was an interesting time.
   5 My brother travelled to South America _____ year.
   6 I started my new job _____ 4 November.
   7 My grandfather played football for Arsenal 50 years _____ .
   8 I usually finish work early _____ Friday.

◀ Go back to page 65

## VOCABULARY PRACTICE

## 8A Traffic verbs

1 ▶ 8.1 Listen and repeat.

 1 **book** a flight
 2 **fly**
 3 **get in** a taxi
 4 **get lost**
 5 **get off** a bus
 6 **get on** a train
 7 **get out of** a taxi
 8 **miss** the bus
 9 **ride** a bike
 10 **sail**
 11 **take** the underground
 12 **walk**

2 Tick (✓) the verbs we can use with each type of transport.

|  | a taxi | a bike | a boat | a plane | a bus | a train |
|---|---|---|---|---|---|---|
| ride |  |  |  |  |  |  |
| take |  |  |  |  |  |  |
| miss |  |  |  |  |  |  |
| get in / out of |  |  |  |  |  |  |
| get on / off |  |  |  |  |  |  |
| sail |  |  |  |  |  |  |

3 Choose the correct words to complete the sentences.

1 Anne needs to *walk / book* a ticket for her trip to Los Angeles.
2 This is our bus stop. Quick, *get off / get out* now!
3 Let's *walk / get out* home. It's a nice warm evening.
4 Juan decided to *sail / fly* to Spain because he hates planes.
5 When the train arrived, a lot of people tried to *get lost / get on*.
6 There aren't any trains. We need to *ride / take* a taxi home.
7 They *missed / booked* their bus, so they arrived really late.
8 I can drive you home if you want. *Get in / Get out*!
9 Stuart *drives / rides* a motorbike because it's fast.
10 You can *take / ride* the number 35 bus to the city centre.

◀ Go back to page 68

125

VOCABULARY PRACTICE

## 8B Weather and seasons

1 ▶ 8.6 Listen and repeat.

1 hot
2 warm
3 cold
4 cloudy
5 sunny
6 wet
7 dry
8 windy
9 foggy
10 rain
11 snow
12 spring
13 summer
14 autumn
15 winter

**Look!** *rain* and *snow* are verbs. To talk about the weather now, we say *It's raining/It's snowing*. To talk about the weather in general, we say *It rains/It snows*.

2 Look at the weather map and complete the sentences.

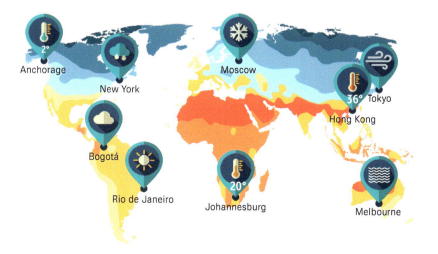

1 It's _____ in Moscow.
2 It's _____ in Bogotá.
3 It's _____ in Rio de Janeiro.
4 It's _____ in New York.
5 It's _____ in Tokyo.
6 It's _____ in Hong Kong.
7 It's _____ in Anchorage.
8 It's _____ in Johannesburg.
9 It's _____ in Melbourne.

◀ Go back to page 70

**VOCABULARY PRACTICE**

## 8C Nature

1 ▶ 8.7 Listen and repeat.

1 beach
2 cloud
3 field
4 flower
5 forest
6 grass
7 mountain
8 river
9 sea
10 sky
11 sun
12 tree

2 Choose the correct words to complete the sentences.

1 Kilimanjaro is a *beach* / *mountain* in Tanzania.
2 The Nile is a *river* / *field* in Africa.
3 The Amazon is a type of *forest* / *mountain* in South America.
4 The rose is a *cloud* / *flower* that can be different colours.
5 Jamaica is in the Caribbean *Sea* / *River*.
6 Copacabana is a *beach* / *forest* in Brazil.
7 Apples are a fruit that come from a *grass* / *tree*.
8 The temperature of the *sun* / *sky* is 15 million °C.
9 Cumulus, Cirrus and Stratus are *clouds* / *trees*.
10 Animals like horses and rabbits eat *trees* / *grass*.

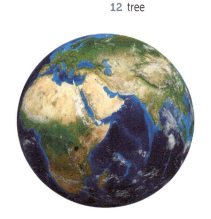

◀ Go back to page 72

127

# VOCABULARY PRACTICE

## 9A Clothes

1 ▶ 9.1 Listen and repeat.

1 belt
2 boots
3 coat
4 dress
5 hat
6 jacket
7 jeans
8 jumper
9 shirt
10 shoes
11 skirt
12 socks
13 suit
14 T-shirt
15 trousers

2 Write the clothes from exercise 1 in the correct places.

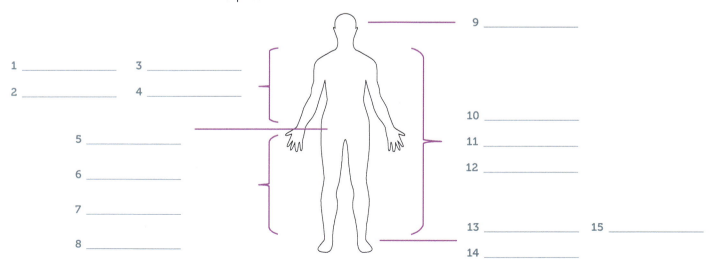

◀ Go back to page 78

VOCABULARY PRACTICE

## 9B Feelings

1  9.6 Listen and repeat.

1 angry

2 bored

3 calm

4 excited

5 happy

6 hungry

7 sad

8 scared

9 surprised

10 thirsty

11 tired

12 worried

2 Choose the correct adjective to complete the sentences.
1 Can I have a drink of water? I'm really *hungry* / *thirsty*.
2 He's *surprised* / *worried* about money because he doesn't have a job.
3 I'm *bored* / *scared*. This film isn't very interesting.
4 It's Louisa's birthday tomorrow – she's very *excited* / *tired*.
5 I like yoga because it makes me feel *calm* / *sad*.
6 Are you *angry* / *hungry*? Do you want a sandwich?
7 You're very *scared* / *tired*. Why don't you go to bed?
8 Tim is *angry* / *hungry* with me because I broke his computer.
9 I was *bored* / *surprised* that John ran a marathon because he doesn't like sport.
10 Suzie doesn't like horror films. They make her feel *scared* / *surprised*.

3 Match the feelings in the box with the messages.

tired    sad    worried    angry    surprised

1 **Julia** I get my exam results today! 😬

2 **Ying-Li** I arrived in London today after a 10-hour flight. 😴

3 **Saanvi** I won the Science competition. I can't believe it! 😱

4 **Dave** All my friends are in Cuba on holiday. I'm at work. 😣

5 **Hans** I lost my wallet on the train today … and I was late for work. 😠

◀ Go back to page 80

129

VOCABULARY PRACTICE

## 9C Shopping

1  ▶ 9.12 Listen and repeat.

1 buy a car

2 go shopping

3 pay by credit card

4 pay with cash

5 sell ice cream

6 shop online

7 spend money

8 try on clothes

9 department store

10 local shops

11 market

12 shopping centre

2  Match the halves to make sentences.

1 I always pay by _____
2 We usually spend _____
3 Can I try on _____
4 I never shop _____
5 Jorge sells _____
6 Malika wants to buy _____
7 You can only pay with _____
8 We need to go _____

a these jeans, please?
b a new laptop.
c fish in the market.
d shopping for food.
e £100 every weekend.
f credit card. It's easy!
g cash in this shop.
h online. I like real shops.

3  Choose the correct words to complete the sentences.

1 I don't *go* / *buy* shopping on Saturdays. There are lots of people.
2 My brother works for a technology company. He *spends* / *sells* computers.
3 Sharon lives in a small village. There are only three or four *department stores* / *local shops*.
4 Carla *spends* / *buys* all her money on clothes.
5 When we go on holiday, we usually pay *with* / *by* credit card.
6 The *shopping centre* / *market* near us has a cinema and lots of restaurants.
7 I always *try* / *shop* on clothes before I buy them.
8 My mobile phone is broken. I need to *buy* / *pay* a new one.

130  ◀ Go back to page 82

**VOCABULARY PRACTICE**

## 10A  Free-time activities

1   ▶ 10.1 Listen and repeat.

1 go to a concert

2 go to a festival

3 go to the beach

4 have a barbecue

5 have a good time

6 have a party

7 stay at home

8 stay in a hotel

9 stay in a tent

10 visit a museum

11 visit an art gallery

12 visit family/friends

13 watch a film

14 watch a football match

15 watch a video

2  Match the activities in the box with the people.

> visit family    go to the beach    have a barbecue    watch a film
> have a party    stay at home    visit a museum    stay in a tent

1 Erica likes hot weather and swimming. She has two new books to read.
2 It's a nice sunny day. Paul is hungry and he has some meat and fish.
3 It's Lucia's birthday tomorrow and she wants to celebrate with her friends.
4 The weather isn't good and Samuel has an exam next week.
5 Marek and Kasia are in London for the weekend. They're interested in history.
6 Sonia loves nature. She wants to go on holiday, but she doesn't want to spend a lot of money.
7 Cristian is going to San Francisco. His parents and brothers and sisters live there.
8 Natalia is at home tonight. She bought a new 102 cm TV last week.

◀ Go back to page 86

131

## VOCABULARY PRACTICE

## 10B Types of music and film

1  ▶ 10.9 Listen and repeat.

1 classical music

2 electronic music

3 hip-hop music

4 jazz music

5 pop music

6 rock music

7 an action film

8 a comedy

9 a drama

10 a horror film

11 a romance

12 a science-fiction film

2  Look at the pictures and write the types of music and films.

1 _____

2 _____

3 _____

4 _____

5 _____

6 _____

◀ Go back to page 88

**VOCABULARY PRACTICE**

## 10C Sports and games

1 ▶ 10.10 Listen and repeat.

1 do gymnastics

2 do karate

3 do Pilates

4 do yoga

5 go cycling

6 go rock climbing

7 go running

8 go skiing

9 go swimming

10 go walking

11 play basketball

12 play chess

13 play football

14 play hockey

15 play rugby

16 play tennis

17 play videogames

18 play volleyball

**Look!**
We use *play* with sports that use a ball and with games.
*I play golf.*

We use *go* with activities that end in *-ing*.
*I go sailing.*

We use *do* with individual activities and sports that don't use a ball.
*I do judo.*

2 Complete the sentences with the correct form of *go*, *play* or *do*.

1 He usually _____ tennis at the weekend.
2 It's a lovely sunny day. Why don't we _____ walking?
3 They _____ gymnastics every Monday after school.
4 Do you want to _____ chess later?
5 Did you _____ cycling last weekend?
6 She often _____ Pilates to relax.
7 I _____ skiing with my parents every winter.
8 Do your children _____ a lot of videogames?

◀ Go back to page 90

133

COMMUNICATION PRACTICE

## Hello  Student A

1  Look at the labels. Ask Student B for the name of the city.
   A *What's LHR?*
   B *I think it's London.*
   A *How do you spell that?*
   B *L-O-N-D-O-N.*

2  Listen to Student B's airport codes. Tell him/her the correct city for the letters.

   New Delhi   Cape Town   Barcelona   New York   Amsterdam

FINAL DEST. **LHR**  1 _____
FINAL DEST. **MEX**  2 _____
FINAL DEST. **IST**  3 _____
FINAL DEST. **LAX**  4 _____
FINAL DEST. **HGK**  5 _____

## 1A  Student A

1  You are Mehmet. Answer Student B's questions with the information.
   B *What's your name?*
   A *I'm Mehmet Guliyev.*
   B *How do you spell that?*
   A *M-E-H-M-E-T ...*

   | Name: | Mehmet Guliyev |
   | Nationality: | Turkish |
   | Phone: | 90 312 213 2965 |

2  Ask Student B the questions and write down his/her answers.
   1  What's your name?
      _____
   2  Where are you from?
      _____
   3  What's your phone number?
      _____

## 1C  Student A

1  Ask Student B questions about the Antarctic Zebras to complete the information.

   *Where are they from?   How old is Bev?   What is her job?*

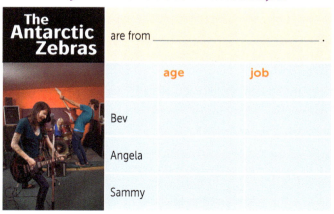

The Antarctic Zebras are from _____ .

| | age | job |
|---|---|---|
| Bev | | |
| Angela | | |
| Sammy | | |

2  Now look at the information about the Rocking Stones. Answer Student B's questions.

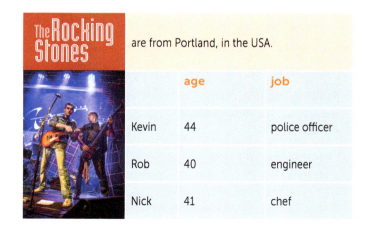

The Rocking Stones are from Portland, in the USA.

| | age | job |
|---|---|---|
| Kevin | 44 | police officer |
| Rob | 40 | engineer |
| Nick | 41 | chef |

COMMUNICATION PRACTICE

## 2A Students A and B

1 Look at the picture. In pairs, ask about the objects.
   *What's this/that?   What are these/those?*
2 Now go to page 143 and check your ideas.

## 2C Student A

Ask and answer questions with Student B to complete David and Victoria Beckham's family tree.

A *What's David's mother's name?*
B *Her name is …*

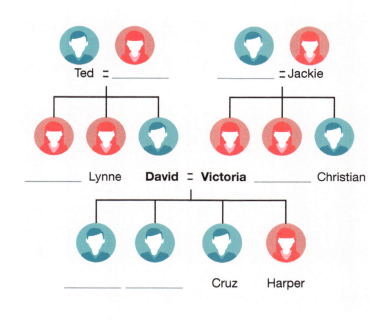

## 2D Student A

1 Ask Student B the questions and write down the answers. Remember to be polite.

   A *Excuse me, what time's the next train to Boston, please?*
   B *It's at quarter to twelve.*
   A *Thanks.*
   1 What time's the next train to Boston? _____
   2 What's Lucy's phone number? _____
   3 Where's the teacher from? _____
   4 How old are you? _____
   5 What's the name of the café? _____

2 Answer Student B's questions with the answers in the box.

   He's 28.   She's from Mexico.   You're in Room 48.
   It's F-O-S-T-E-R.   It's at 6.40.

135

# COMMUNICATION PRACTICE

## 3A  Student A

1  Ask Student B questions to complete the information.
   A  *What do you have for breakfast?*
   B  *For breakfast, I eat ...*

| breakfast | lunch | dinner |
|-----------|-------|--------|
|           |       |        |

2  Look at the information. Answer Student B's questions about your breakfast, lunch and dinner.

## 3C  Student A

1  Ask Student B questions about Magda to complete the information in the table.

   A  *Does Magda live in a city?*
   B  *Yes, she does. She lives in Gdansk.*

|                              | Magda | Antonio |
|------------------------------|-------|---------|
| work in an office?           |       | ✗ (he / work / in a school) |
| live in a city?              |       | ✓ |
| have children?               |       | ✓ (he / have / two daughters) |
| watch TV in the morning?     |       | ✗ (he / work) |
| use public transport every day? |    | ✓ |
| go to the gym after work?    |       | ✗ (he / make / dinner) |
| study in the evening?        |       | ✗ (he / watch / TV) |
| do sport at the weekend?     |       | ✓ |

2  Look at the information about Antonio. Answer Student B's questions and give extra information when you can.
   B  *Does Antonio work in an office?*    A  *No, he doesn't. He works in a school.*

## 4A  Student A

1  Write sentences in the present simple with the adverbs of frequency in brackets. Then read them to Student B.

   1  Leila / watch / films on her phone. (sometimes)
   _____
   2  Dean / wake up / before 6.00 a.m. (often)
   _____
   3  Paulo / read / in bed. (usually)
   _____
   4  Marta / be / late for work. (never)
   _____
   5  Shaun / cook / dinner for his family. (always)
   _____

2  Listen to Student B. Match the names in the box with the people.

   Danny   Nina   Eric   Claire   Tom

1 _____  2 _____  3 _____  4 _____  5 _____

*I usually finish work after 7.00 p.m.*   *I'm often in the library at night.*   *I always drink tea for breakfast.*   *I never have a bath in the morning.*   *I sometimes go to the gym on Saturday.*

**COMMUNICATION PRACTICE**

## 4C Student A

1 Ask Student B questions about Ella. Write his/her answers.

A *Where does Ella live?*  B *She lives in Manchester.*

**Ella**

**Questions**
Where / live?
What / do?
Where / work?
What time / get up?
What time / finish work?
Why / like her job?
How / relax in the evening?
What / do at the weekend?

2 Read Zain's profile. Listen to Student B and answer his/her questions.

**Zain**

Hi, I'm Zain. I live in Los Angeles. I'm a waiter at a big hotel in Hollywood. I get up at 8.00 a.m. and before work I usually go to the gym. I start work at 11.00 and I finish at 9.00 p.m. I like my job because I meet interesting people. To relax in the evening, I play the guitar. I usually work at the weekend.

## 4D Student A

1 You are a customer. Ask Student B for the things on your shopping list. Then ask how much each thing is. Remember to be polite.

A *Good morning. Can I have a cheese sandwich, please?*
B *Here you are.*
A *Thank you. How much is it?*
B *£1.99. Anything else?*

Shopping list
1 cheese sandwich
6 eggs
some orange juice
some coffee
some pasta
Total price = ?

2 You are a shop assistant. Serve Student B. Remember to be polite.

```
2x bottles water      $1.60
fish                  $5.80
1x pizza (4 cheese)   $3.99
1 box salad           $1.50
1 chocolate cake      $3.85
Total                $16.74
```

## 5A Student A

1 Look at the table. Ask questions with *can* to guess which person Student B has.

A *Can she drive?*
B *Yes, she can.*

|  | Annie | Mona | Sara | Lucy | Hana | Kim |
|---|---|---|---|---|---|---|
| Can / drive? | ✗ | ✓ | ✓ | ✓ | ✓ | ✓ |
| Can / speak Spanish? | ✗ | ✓ | ✓ | ✗ | ✓ | ✗ |
| Can / play the guitar? | ✓ | ✗ | ✓ | ✗ | ✓ | ✗ |
| Can / cook Chinese food? | ✓ | ✓ | ✗ | ✓ | ✗ | ✗ |
| Can / dance salsa? | ✗ | ✗ | ✓ | ✗ | ✗ | ✓ |

2 Answer Student B's questions about Mark. You can only say *Yes, he can* or *No, he can't*.

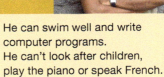

He can swim well and write computer programs.
He can't look after children, play the piano or speak French.

# COMMUNICATION PRACTICE

## 5C Student A

1 Look at the profiles for a website called *New Friends*. Ask and answer questions with Student B to complete the information.

A *What does Daniela think about cooking?*   B *She likes it.*

☺☺ = love, ☺ = like, ☹ = not like, ☹☹ = hate

| **Daniela** | | **Bill** | | **Monica** | |
|---|---|---|---|---|---|
| | cooking | | walking | | going out |
| | cats and dogs | | housework | | cycling |
| | early mornings | | books | | the cinema |

| **Miguel** | | **Claudio** | | **Lucy** | |
|---|---|---|---|---|---|
| ☹ | cleaning | ☺ | swimming | ☺ | sleeping |
| ☺☺ | reading | ☺☺ | watching films | ☺ | animals |
| ☹☹ | sport | ☹ | dancing | ☺☺ | food and drink |

2 Look at the profiles again. Find the best new friend for each person.

## 6A Student A

Look at the picture. Ask and answer questions with Student B to find six differences.

A *Are there any hotels?*
B *Yes, there are. There are two hotels.*
A *In my picture, there's one hotel.*
B *Is there a cinema?*

## 6C Student A

1 Describe your picture to Student B. He/She will draw it.

A *There's a bed. Next to the bed, there's a small table.*

2 Listen to Student B and draw the room.

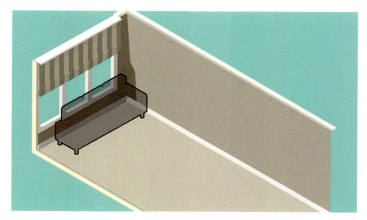

**COMMUNICATION PRACTICE**

## 6D Student A

1 Ask Student B for directions to the places in the box. Listen and mark on the map where they are. Check the information if you need to.

| post office   bank   Internet café |

A *Excuse me, is there a post office near here?*
B *Yes, there is. You go down Market Street …*
A *Could you repeat that, please?*

2 Listen to Student B. Look at the map and give directions.

## 7A Student A

1 Ask Student B questions with *was* to match the celebrities with their jobs and where they were from.

A *Was Federico Fellini an artist?*
B *No, he wasn't.*

1 Federico Fellini    writer    South Africa
2 Janis Joplin    politician    the USA
3 Nelson Mandela    film director    Colombia
4 Greta Garbo    artist    Japan
5 Katsushika Hokusai    singer    Italy
6 Gabriel García Márquez    actor    Sweden

2 Answer Student B's questions about the celebrities. You can only say *Yes, he/she was* or *No, he/she wasn't.*

1 Frida Kahlo was an artist from Mexico.
2 Johan Cruyff was a footballer from the Netherlands.
3 Celia Cruz was a singer from Cuba.
4 Jane Austen was a writer from the UK.
5 Paco de Lucía was a musician from Spain.
6 Jawaharlal Nehru was a politician from India.

## 7C Student A

1 Ask Student B questions. Find one incorrect piece of information for each person.

A *Did Luke visit his grandparents last week?*
B *No, he didn't. He visited his grandparents last month.*

1 Luke / visit / his grandparents / last ~~week~~    month
2 Kenny / travel / to Brazil / three years ago
3 Clara / play / volleyball / yesterday
4 Debbie / cook / noodles / last night
5 Steve / work / as a teacher / in the 1980s
6 Amelia / watch / a TV show / yesterday morning

2 Listen to Student B's questions. Correct the information.

1 Zoe stayed in a hotel in the city centre last year.
2 Jim studied Spanish at university in the 1990s.
3 Antonia walked 30 kilometres yesterday.
4 Leandro watched a football match three days ago.
5 Rachel started a new job in London last month.
6 Tom finished work one hour ago.

## 7A London's famous houses: answers

1 Mahatma Gandhi

2 Bob Marley

3 Agatha Christie

4 Vincent van Gogh

COMMUNICATION PRACTICE

## 8A Student A

1 Ask Student B questions to find out what Lola did yesterday.

   A *Where did Lola go?*
   B *She went to her dad's birthday party.*

2 Read the information and answer Student B's questions about what Mateo did yesterday.

**Lola**

| Where / go? |
| What time / leave / the house? |
| she / take / the bus? |
| What / wear? |
| What / buy / for her dad? |
| she / have / a good time? |
| Where / sleep / last night? |

**Mateo**

| He / go / Rome |
| He / fly |
| He / take / taxi to the airport |
| His flight / leave at 11.00 a.m. |
| He / go / with friends |
| He / sleep / on a plane for 20 minutes |
| He / have / a good journey |

## 8C Student A

1 Look at the picture for one minute. Then close your book and answer Student B's questions.

2 Give Student B one minute to look at his/her picture. Ask him/her questions with *Was/Were there a/an/any …?* and the words in the box. If he/she answers *Yes, there were*, ask *How many were there?*

| boats | hospital | cars | flowers |
| birds | shops | beach | river |

A *Were there any boats?*   B *Yes, there were.*
A *How many were there?*   B *There was one boat.*

## 8D Student A

1 Read the situation in the box, then look at the flowchart. You are the receptionist. Student B calls you. Have the conversation.

   A *Hello, Green Lane Medical Centre. Jorge speaking. How can I help you?*
   B *Hello, my name's Anna Lopez. I'd like to see the doctor.*

> You work at the Green Lane Medical Centre. Answer the phone. Ask the person what the problem is.

**Receptionist**

- Answer the phone. Give the name of the medical centre/sports centre and your name.
- Ask more detailed questions.
- Ask for the caller's contact details.
- Finish the call.

**Patient/Customer**

- Introduce yourself and say why you are calling.
- Answer.
- Answer.

2 Read the situation in the box, then look at the flowchart again. You are the customer. Call Student B and have the conversation.

> You want to join a sports centre. You're interested in swimming and tennis.
> Your phone number is 07700 900382.

**COMMUNICATION PRACTICE**

## 9C  Student A

Ask and answer the question *How often do/does …?* with Student B to complete the table.

A *How often do Jon and Andy go to the cinema?*
B *They go to the cinema three or four times a year.*

| Laura | have dinner in a restaurant | twice a month |
| Jon and Andy | go to the cinema | |
| Carlota | shop online | once or twice a week |
| Ahmed | ride a motorbike | |
| Hope and Sara | check their emails | four or five times a day |
| Igor | read a new book | |
| Luisa and Raul | go swimming | every week |
| Yannis | go on holiday | |

## 10A  Student A

Look at your diary. Try to find a time when you can meet Student B. Ask and answer the question *What are you doing on …?* for the different days.

A *What are you doing on Monday morning?*
B *I'm going to the gym. What about Monday afternoon?*

| | Monday | Tuesday | Wednesday | Thursday | Friday |
|---|---|---|---|---|---|
| Morning | | | travel to the city | | |
| Afternoon | see doctor | have lunch with parents | visit National Museum | | |
| Evening | watch film at cinema | | stay with friends | | have dinner with Carl |

## 10C  Student A

Ask Student B questions about his/her hobby in the correct tense. Write down his/her answers. Then guess what the hobby is.

A *How often do you do your hobby?*
B *I do it twice a week.*

**Student B's hobby**

**Your hobby: rock climbing**

1  How often / you / do / your hobby?     Every weekend.
2  When / you / start?     When I was 14.
3  it / be / expensive?     No, it isn't.
4  it / be / dangerous?     It can be.
5  you / play / it in a team?     No, but I always go with another person.
6  How many people / be there / in your team?     –
7  Where / you / do / your hobby?     Sometimes at a sports centre, sometimes in the mountains.
8  you / do / your hobby next weekend?     Yes, I'm driving to the beach on Friday night.

COMMUNICATION PRACTICE

# Hello Student B

1 Listen to Student A's airport codes. Tell him/her the correct city for the letters.

| Hong Kong   Los Angeles   Mexico City   London   Istanbul |

A *What's LHR?*
B *I think it's London.*
A *How do you spell that?*
B *L-O-N-D-O-N.*

2 Look at the labels. Ask Student A for the name of the city.

1 _____  2 _____  3 _____

4 _____  5 _____

# 1A Student B

1 Ask Student A the questions and write down his/her answers.
   1 What's your name?
   _____
   2 Where are you from?
   _____
   3 What's your phone number?
   _____

2 You are Saori. Answer Student A's questions with the information.

A *What's your name?*
B *I'm Saori Arakawa.*
A *How do you spell that?*
B *S-A-O-R-I …*

| Name: | Saori Arakawa |
| Nationality: | Japanese |
| Phone: | 81 90 1790 1357 |

# 1C Student B

1 Look at the information about the Antarctic Zebras. Answer Student A's questions.

are from Liverpool, in the UK.

| | age | job |
|---|---|---|
| Bev | 19 | student |
| Angela | 24 | IT worker |
| Sammy | 25 | tour guide |

2 Now ask Student A questions about the Rocking Stones to complete the information.

*Where are they from?   How old is Kevin?   What is his job?*

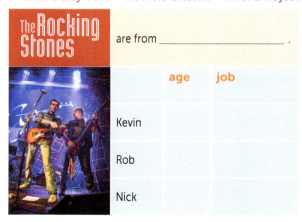

are from _____ .

| | age | job |
|---|---|---|
| Kevin | | |
| Rob | | |
| Nick | | |

142

COMMUNICATION PRACTICE

## 2A Students A and B

Look at the picture. In pairs, discuss if you were right or wrong.

A *This is a pen.*
B *You're right.*

## 2C Student B

Ask and answer questions with Student A to complete David and Victoria Beckham's family tree.

B *What's Victoria's mother's name?*
A *Her name is ....*

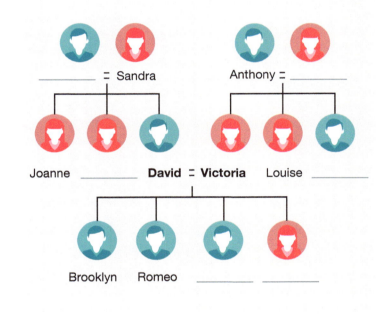

## 2D Student B

1 Answer Student A's questions with the answers in the box.

> I'm 39.  It's 07700 900638.  The Oak Tree Café.
> It's at 11.45.  He's from Canada.

2 Ask Student A the questions and write down the answers. Remember to be polite.

B *Excuse me, what time's the flight to Los Angeles, please?*
A *It's at twenty to seven.*
B *Thanks.*
1 What time's the flight to Los Angeles? _____
2 How old is the teacher? _____
3 Where's María from? _____
4 What room am I in? _____
5 How do you spell your surname? _____

143

# COMMUNICATION PRACTICE

## 3A Student B

1 Look at the information. Answer Student A's questions about your breakfast, lunch and dinner.

2 Ask Student A questions to complete the information.

B *What do you have for breakfast?*
A *For breakfast, I eat …*

| breakfast | lunch | dinner |
|---|---|---|
|  |  |  |

## 3C Student B

1 Look at the information about Magda. Answer Student A's questions and give extra information when you can.

A *Does Magda live in a city?*
B *Yes, she does. She lives in Gdansk.*

|  | Magda | Antonio |
|---|---|---|
| work in an office? | ✓ |  |
| live in a city? | ✓ (she / live / in Gdansk) |  |
| have children? | ✗ (she / have / two cats) |  |
| watch TV in the morning? | ✗ |  |
| use public transport every day? | ✗ (she / walk / to work) |  |
| go to the gym after work? | ✓ |  |
| study in the evening? | ✓ (she / study / English) |  |
| do sport at the weekend? | ✗ (she / make / cakes) |  |

2 Ask Student A questions about Antonio to complete the information in the table.

B *Does Antonio work in an office?*   A *No, he doesn't. He works in a school.*

## 4A Student B

1 Listen to Student A. Match the names in the box with the people.

Marta  Shaun  Leila  Dean  Paulo

1 _____  2 _____  3 _____  4 _____  5 _____

*I often wake up before 6.00 a.m.*

*I'm never late for work.*

*I usually read in bed.*

*I sometimes watch films on my phone.*

*I always cook dinner for my family.*

2 Make sentences in the present simple with the adverbs of frequency in brackets. Then read them to Student A.

1 Claire / drink / tea for breakfast. (always)
_____

2 Tom / go / to the gym on Saturday. (sometimes)
_____

3 Eric / have / a bath in the morning. (never)
_____

4 Danny / be / in the library at night. (often)
_____

5 Nina / finish / work after 7.00 p.m. (usually)
_____

COMMUNICATION PRACTICE

## 4C Student B

1 Read Ella's profile. Listen to Student A and answer his/her questions.

   A *Where does Ella live?*   B *She lives in Manchester.*

2 Ask Student A questions about Zain. Write his/her answers.

**Ella**

Hi, I'm Ella. I live in Manchester. I'm a teacher at a school in the city centre. I usually get up at 6.00 a.m. I start work at 8.30 and I finish at 5.00 p.m. I love my job because I like children. To relax in the evening, I watch TV with my family. At the weekend, I do a lot of sport.

**Zain**

| Questions |
|---|
| Where / live? |
| What / do? |
| Where / work? |
| What time / get up? |
| What time / finish work? |
| Why / like his job? |
| How / relax in the evening? |
| What / do at the weekend? |

## 4D Student B

1 You are a shop assistant. Serve Student A. Remember to be polite.

   A *Good morning. Can I have a cheese sandwich, please?*
   B *Here you are.*
   A *Thank you. How much is it?*
   B *£1.99. Anything else?*

```
1 sandwich (cheese)   £1.99
6 eggs                £2.50
orange juice          £1.80
coffee                £3.29
pasta                 £1.50
Total                £11.08
```

2 You are a customer. Ask Student A for the things on your shopping list. Then ask how much each thing is. Remember to be polite.

```
Shopping list
2 bottles of water
some fish
1 four-cheese pizza
1 box of salad
1 chocolate cake
Total price = ?
```

## 5A Student B

1 Answer Student A's questions about Hana. You can only say *Yes, she can* or *No, she can't*.

   A *Can she drive?*
   B *Yes, she can.*

**HANA**

She can drive, speak Spanish and play the guitar.
She can't cook Chinese food or dance salsa.

2 Look at the table. Ask questions with *can* to guess which person Student A has.

|  | Sergio | Tom | Mark | Andy | Pete | Dennis |
|---|---|---|---|---|---|---|
| Can / look after children? | ✓ | ✗ | ✗ | ✗ | ✓ | ✗ |
| Can / swim well? | ✗ | ✓ | ✓ | ✗ | ✓ | ✓ |
| Can / play the piano? | ✗ | ✗ | ✗ | ✗ | ✓ | ✗ |
| Can / speak French? | ✓ | ✓ | ✗ | ✓ | ✗ | ✗ |
| Can / write computer programs? | ✗ | ✗ | ✓ | ✗ | ✓ | ✗ |

145

# COMMUNICATION PRACTICE

## 5C Student B

1 Look at the profiles for a website called *New Friends*. Ask and answer questions with Student A to complete the information.

B *What does Miguel think about cleaning?*  A *He doesn't like it.*

☺☺ = love, ☺ = like, ☹ = not like, ☹☹ = hate

**Daniela**
| ☺ | cooking |
| ☺☺ | cats and dogs |
| ☹ | early mornings |

**Bill**
| ☹ | walking |
| ☹☹ | housework |
| ☺ | books |

**Monica**
| ☹ | going out |
| ☹ | cycling |
| ☺ | the cinema |

**Miguel**
| | cleaning |
| | reading |
| | sport |

**Claudio**
| | swimming |
| | watching films |
| | dancing |

**Lucy**
| | sleeping |
| | animals |
| | food and drink |

2 Look at the profiles again. Find the best new friend for each person.

## 6A Student B

Look at the picture. Ask and answer questions with Student A to find six differences.

B *Are there any hotels?*
A *Yes, there are. There's one hotel.*
B *In my picture, there are two hotels.*
A *Is there a cinema?*

## 6C Student B

1 Listen to Student A and draw the room.

A *There's a bed. Next to the bed, there's a small table.*

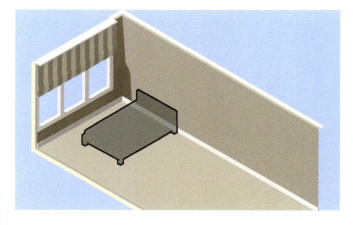

2 Describe your picture to Student A. He/She will draw it.

B *There's a sofa in front of the window.*

146

COMMUNICATION PRACTICE

## 6D  Student B

1  Listen to Student A. Look at the map and give directions.

   A *Excuse me, is there a post office near here?*
   B *Yes, there is. You go down Market Street ...*
   A *Could you repeat that, please?*

2  Ask Student A for directions to the places in the box. Listen and mark on the map where they are. Check the information if you need to.

   restaurant
   tourist information office
   supermarket

## 7A  Student B

1  Answer Student A's questions about the celebrities. You can only say *Yes, he/she was* or *No, he/she wasn't*.

   A *Was Federico Fellini an artist?*
   B *No, he wasn't.*
   1  Federico Fellini was a film director from Italy.
   2  Janis Joplin was a singer from the USA.
   3  Nelson Mandela was a politician from South Africa.
   4  Greta Garbo was an actor from Sweden.
   5  Katsushika Hokusai was an artist from Japan.
   6  Gabriel García Márquez was a writer from Colombia.

2  Ask Student A questions with *was* to match the celebrities with their jobs and where they were from.

   1  Frida Kahlo         footballer    India
   2  Johan Cruyff        musician      Spain
   3  Celia Cruz          politician    Mexico
   4  Jane Austen         singer        the Netherlands
   5  Paco de Lucía       writer        Cuba
   6  Jawaharlal Nehru    artist        the UK

## 7C  Student B

1  Listen to Student A's questions. Correct the information.

   A *Did Luke visit his grandparents last week?*
   B *No, he didn't. He visited his grandparents last month.*
   1  Luke visited his grandparents last month.
   2  Kenny travelled to Brazil six years ago.
   3  Clara played basketball yesterday.
   4  Debbie cooked rice last night.
   5  Steve worked as a teacher in the 1970s.
   6  Amelia watched a film yesterday morning.

2  Ask Student A questions. Find one incorrect piece of information for each person.

   1  Zoe / stay / in a hotel near the beach / last year
   2  Jim / study / German at university / in the 1990s
   3  Antonia / walk / 30 kilometres / two days ago
   4  Leandro / watch / a football match / last week
   5  Rachel / start / a new job in Paris / last month
   6  Tom / finish / work / half an hour ago

## 9C  Questionnaire results

**Mostly as:** You don't like shopping and you hate shopping centres. You prefer to spend money on other things. What do you do and how often do you do it?

**Mostly bs:** You like shopping, but you also like doing other things. A shopping centre is a good place to meet friends. How often do you go there?

**Mostly cs:** You love shopping – it's your life. You go shopping two or three times a week and you shop online almost every day ... but do you really need to buy all those things?

147

## COMMUNICATION PRACTICE

### 8A Student B

1 Read the information and answer Student A's questions about what Lola did yesterday.

A *Where did Lola go?*   B *She went to her dad's birthday party.*

**Lola**
- She / go / her dad's birthday party
- She / leave / the house at 7.00 p.m.
- She / take / the train
- She / wear / a new dress
- She / buy / a book
- She / have / a good time
- She / sleep / on her dad's sofa

2 Ask Student A questions to find out what Mateo did yesterday.

**Mateo**
- Where / he / go?
- he / go / by train?
- he / take / a taxi to the airport?
- what time / his flight / leave?
- he / go / with friends?
- he / sleep / on the plane?
- he / have / a good journey?

### 8C Student B

1 Give Student A one minute to look at his/her picture. Ask him/her questions with *Was/Were there a/an/any ...?* and the words in the box. If he/she answers *Yes, there were*, ask *How many were there?*

| people   clouds   forest   trees |
| bus   houses   cars   river |

B *Were there any people?*   A *Yes, there were.*
B *How many were there?*   A *There were four people.*

2 Look at the picture for one minute. Then close your book and answer Student A's questions.

### 8D Student B

1 Read the situation in the box, then look at the flowchart. You are the patient. Call Student A and have the conversation.

A *Hello, Green Lane Medical Centre. Jorge speaking. How can I help you?*
B *Hello, my name's Anna Lopez. I'd like to see the doctor.*

> You don't feel well and want to see the doctor. Your head hurts. Your phone number is 01632 960785.

**Receptionist**

| Answer the phone. Give the name of the medical centre/sports centre and your name. | → | **Patient/Customer** Introduce yourself and say why you are calling. |
| Ask more detailed questions. | → | Answer. |
| Ask for the caller's contact details. | → | Answer. |
| Finish the call. | | |

2 Read the situation in the box, then look at the flowchart again. You are the receptionist. Student A calls you. Have the conversation.

> You work at a sports centre called The Fitness Factory. Answer the phone. Ask the person what sports they want to do.

COMMUNICATION PRACTICE

## 9A  Student B

Look at the picture. Describe James, Grace and Kara to Student A. Try to find six differences.

B *Grace is wearing a red dress and boots.*
A *In my picture, she's wearing shoes.*

## 9C  Student B

Ask and answer the question *How often do/does ...?* with Student A to complete the table.

B *How often does Laura have dinner in a restaurant?*
A *She has dinner in a restaurant twice a month.*

| Laura | have dinner in a restaurant | |
| Jon and Andy | go to the cinema | three or four times a year |
| Carlota | shop online | |
| Ahmed | ride a motorbike | every day |
| Hope and Sara | check their emails | |
| Igor | read a new book | four or five times a year |
| Luisa and Raul | go swimming | |
| Yannis | go on holiday | once a year |

## 10A  Student B

Look at your diary. Try to find a time when you can meet Student A. Ask and answer the question *What are you doing on ...?* for the different days.

A *What are you doing on Monday morning?*
B *I'm going to the gym. What about Monday afternoon?*

| | Monday | Tuesday | Wednesday | Thursday | Friday |
|---|---|---|---|---|---|
| Morning | go to the gym | meet Simon for coffee | | take bus to city | see dentist |
| Afternoon | | | | visit art gallery | |
| Evening | | go to a concert | | stay in hotel | |

149

COMMUNICATION PRACTICE

## 9A Student A

Look at the picture. Describe Aziz, Oscar and Petra to Student B. Try to find six differences.

A *Aziz is looking at a white hat.*
B *In my picture, he's looking at some sunglasses.*

## 10C Student B

Ask Student A questions about his/her hobby in the correct tense. Write down his/her answers. Then guess what the hobby is.

B *How often do you do your hobby?*
A *I do it every weekend.*

| | Student A's hobby | Your hobby: basketball |
|---|---|---|
| 1 How often / you / do / your hobby? | | Twice a week. |
| 2 When / you / start? | | Last year. |
| 3 it / be / expensive? | | No, it isn't. |
| 4 it / be / dangerous? | | No, it isn't. |
| 5 you / play / it in a team? | | Yes, I do. |
| 6 How many people / be there / in your team? | | 12 (but only five play at the same time). |
| 7 Where / you / do / your hobby? | | At the sports centre. |
| 8 you / do / your hobby next weekend? | | Yes, we're going to Los Angeles for a match. |

## 10D Students A and B

1 Complete the sentences. You can use real information or invent it.

**About me**
In my free time, I often _____ .
My favourite type of music is _____ .

**Last weekend**
I went shopping on Saturday and I bought _____
_____ .
Last weekend, I _____ .

**My holidays**
Last summer, I went to _____ .
When I'm on holiday, I usually _____ .

**My plans**
Next weekend, I'm meeting _____ .
For my next holiday, I'm _____ .

2 Read your sentences in pairs. Respond with interest using the words in the box.

Oh really?   That's interesting.   That sounds good.   Wow, that's amazing!   Cool!   Great!

A *In my free time, I often go skiing in the mountains.*
B *Wow, that's amazing!*

150

# Irregular verbs

| Infinitive | Past simple |
|---|---|
| be | was, were |
| become | became |
| begin | began |
| break | broke |
| bring | brought |
| buy | bought |
| choose | chose |
| come | came |
| cost | cost |
| do | did |
| drink | drank |
| drive | drove |
| eat | ate |
| fall | fell |
| feel | felt |
| find | found |
| fly | flew |
| get | got |
| give | gave |
| go | went |
| have | had |
| hear | heard |
| hold | held |
| hurt | hurt |
| keep | kept |
| know | knew |
| learn | learnt/learned |

| Infinitive | Past simple |
|---|---|
| leave | left |
| lose | lost |
| make | made |
| meet | met |
| pay | paid |
| put | put |
| read (/riːd/) | read (/red/) |
| ride | rode |
| run | ran |
| say | said |
| see | saw |
| sell | sold |
| sit | sat |
| sleep | slept |
| spend | spent |
| speak | spoke |
| stand | stood |
| swim | swam |
| take | took |
| teach | taught |
| tell | told |
| think | thought |
| understand | understood |
| wake | woke |
| wear | wore |
| win | won |
| write | wrote |

# Richmond

58 St Aldates
Oxford
OX1 1ST
United Kingdom

Printed in Brazil
**ISBN:** 978-84-668-2474-3
**CP:** 779427
**DL:** M-10067-2017
© Richmond / Santillana Global S.L. 2018

All rights reserved. No part of this book may be reproduced, stored in a retrieval system or transmitted in any form by any means, electronic, mechanical, photocopying, recording or otherwise, without the prior permission in writing of the Publisher.

**Publishing Director:** Deborah Tricker
**Publisher:** Simone Foster
**Media Publisher:** Sue Ashcroft
**Content Developer:** David Cole-Powney
**Editors:** Sue Jones, Debra Emmett, Tom Hadland, Fiona Hunt
**Proofreaders:** Pippa Mayfield, Shannon Niell, Jamie Bowman
**Design Manager:** Lorna Heaslip
**Cover Design:** This Ain't Rock'n'Roll, London
**Design & Layout:** Lorna Heaslip, emc design Ltd.
**Photo Researcher:** Magdalena Mayo
*Learning Curve* **video:** Mannic Media
**Audio production:** Tom, Dick and Debbie
**App development:** The Distance

**We would also like to thank the following people for their valuable contribution to writing and developing the material:**
Pamela Vittorio (Video Script Writer), Belen Fernandez (App Project Manager), Eleanor Clements (App Content Creator)

**We would like to thank all those who have given their kind permission to reproduce material for this book:**

**Illustrators:**
Simon Clare; Guillaume Gennet c/o Lemonade; John Goodwin; Sean Longcroft c/o KJA Artists; The Boy Fitzhammond c/o NB Illustration Ltd.

**Photos:**
J. Escandell.com; J. Jaime; J. Lucas; S. Enríquez; 123RF; ALAMY/GerryRousseau, Jim Corwin, Moviestore collection Ltd, Simon Reddy, Stephen French, IanDagnall Computing, Joern Sackermann, dpa picture alliance, Serhii Kucher, ZUMA Press, Inc., All Canada Photos, London Entertainment, Everett Collection Inc, imageBROKER, Pongpun Ampawa, Peter Noyce GBR, Ian Allenden, AF archive, Elizabeth Livermore, Lex Rayton, Ted Foxx, Alvey & Towers Picture Library, Elizabeth Wake, Kristoffer Tripplaar, Lucas Vallecillos, Joe Fairs, Dinodia Photos, Peter D Noyce, Brigette Supernova, Pictorial Press Ltd, Collection Christophel, Jonathan Goldberg, Paul Hastie, Tierfotoagentur, REUTERS, Viktor Fischer, Art of Food, Andrey Armyagov, Alex Ramsay, Blend Images, B Christopher, Judith Collins, David Cabrera Navarro, Roman Tiraspolsky, robertharding, Michael Neelon(misc), Fredrik Kippe, Oleksiy Maksymenko Photography, Patti McConville, D. Callcut, Matthew Taylor, Rafael Angel Irusta Machin, Igor Kovalchuk, MallorcaImages, Paul Quayle, Jozef Polc, Mick Sinclair, Michael Willis, Hugh Threlfall, ITAR-TASS Photo Agency, Bailey-Cooper Photography, jeremy sutton-hibbert, creativep, James Jeffrey Taylor, Oleksiy Maksymenko, Paul Smith, David Levenson, United Archives GmbH, Justin Kase zsixz, Simon Dack, Jeremy Pembrey, Barry Diomede, Alex Linch, Tomas Abad, Valentin Luggen, Sergey Soldatov, Iakov Filimonov, Anton Gvozdikov, Alex Segre, MBI, Paul Gibson, Stocksolutions, MEDIUM FORMAT COLLECTION/Balan Madhavan, allesalltag, David Robertson, Dmytro Zinkevych, Simon Dack News, Vaidas Bucys; CATERS NEWS AGENCY; FOCOLTONE; GETTY IMAGES SALES SPAIN/bjdlzx, Yuri_Arcurs, Reenya, Nikada, Paul Almasy, Martin Rose, Maskot, JamieB, Annie Engel, Fosin2, Darumo, BraunS, artisticco, ajr_images, Bison_, AzmanL, artursfoto, pringletta, Dobino, Berezka_Klo, Indeed, Hero Images, KingWu, Tom Merton, NI QIN, Sam Edwards, Portra, ajaykampani, bgblue, leungchopan, c_kawi, s-c-s, kali9, SensorSpot, LeoPatrizi, Talaj, Pix11, Neyya, Dan Dalton, Chimpinski, DKart, shank_ali, Chris Ryan, londoneye, kickstand, kiankhoon, joto, Fuse, skynesher, asbe, gavran333, Zinkevych, KJA, AFP, ViewStock, John Lund/Sam Diephuis, Hiya Images/Corbis/VCG, Tom Dulat, vm, imaginima, TF-Images, Ben Pipe Photography, Ridofranz, PPcavalry, Edda Dupree / EyeEm, Dave Hogan/MTV 2016, Lightcome, Isovector, VikramRaghuvanshi, FaraFaran, Cimmerian, Bet_Noire, David C Tomlinson, Dave & Les Jacobs, unaemlag, technotr, Zoran Kolundzija, tarras79, stockcam, MacLife Magazine, Jetta Productions, Maya Karkalicheva, DGLimages, innovatedcaptures, FatCamera, Power Sport Images, Jasmina81, Lorraine Boogich, Mirrorpix, Kevin C. Cox - FIFA, Purestock, Caiaimage/Tom Merton, Stockbyte, Jason England / EyeEm, Ted Soqui, scyther5, Steven Swinnen / EyeEm, Weedezign, Westend61, Dave and Les Jacobs/Kolostock, chachamal, Cultura RM Exclusive/Frank and Helena, Echo, imagotres, julief514, karandaev, kpalimski, demaerre, Danny Martindale, Art-Y, omda_info, colematt, clubfoto, Allan Tannenbaum, DNY59, stevecoimages, David Lees, DonNichols, JB Lacroix, asiseeit, Tuutikka, Tarzhanova, Thinkstock, Vladimir Godnik, Uwe Krejci, Venturelli, VladTeodor, Synergee, NurPhoto, Samuel de Roman, nycshooter, RuslanDashinsky, sorincolac, AndreyPopov, AngiePhotos, MistikaS, JGalione, Choreograph, Fotoplanner, Leah Puttkammer, Hero images, John Keeble, Liam Norris, JANIFEST, LWA/Dann Tardif, Ron Galella, Rose_Carson, IvanMiladinovic, Shana Novak, Simon Sarin, T3 Magazine, Floortje, Hung_Chung_Chih, artlensfoto, domin_domin, Frank van Delft, macrovector, michaeljung, penguenstok, Flashpop, DenisKot, Wavebreakmedia, Creative, Claudiad, Sheikoevgeniya, Philipp Nemenz, Bettmann, Al Freni, EmirMemedovski, wir0man, pshonka, Anthony Harvey, Anadolu Agency, mrak_hr, mixetto, i love images, mbbirdy, kivoart, SnegiriBureau, Rick Friedman, jsnover, iconeer, Monty Rakusen, gilaxia, Maksim Ozerov, gerenme, MStudioImages, MATJAZ SLANIC, andresr, Jupiterimages, Jon Feingersh, adekvat, Jamie Garbutt, Jack Mitchell, Mark Cuthbert, R-O-M-A, Paras Griffin, Peathegee Inc, Radius Images, Gabriel Rossi, FrozenShutter, blueringmedia, davidcreacion, NuStock, justhavealook, reportman1985, zeljkosantrac, Dougal Waters, David Redfern, Askold Romanov, Digital Vision, Krasyuk, Javier Pierini, Marc Romanelli, Neustockimages, Andersen Ross, Alistair Berg, Steven Puetzer, Todor Tsvetkov, Devonyu, franckreporter, Anthony Charles, Danita Delimont, senkoumelnik, ferrantraite, Chesnot, ersinkisacik, bluejayphoto, NicolasMcComber, Photos.com Plus, Robyn Mackenzie, Astarot, Tony Vaccaro, Santiago Felipe, Tristan Fewings, Tetra Images, dogayusufdokdok, nicoletaionescu, praetorianphoto, vgajic, Sofie Delauw, Birgit R / EyeEm, Christopher Polk, PeopleImages, Henn Photography, KavalenkavaVolha, Kittisak_Taramas, tunart, Mike Coppola, Nicolas McComber, Tatjana Kaufmann, LuisPortugal, christopherarndt, Adrian Weinbrecht, Chris Sattlberger, subjug, JuliarStudio, Juice Images, Jrg Mikus / EyeEm, sturti, Roberto Westbrook, Tanya Constantine, Valery Sharifulin, Jason Hawkes, Image Source, IMAGEMORE Co., Ltd., Jacob Wackerhausen, seb_ra, crossroadscreative, m-imagephotography, DEA PICTURE LIBRARY, Hiroyuki Ito, Erik Isakson, EvgeniyaTiplyashina, Hill Street Studios, lushik, Mondadori Portfolio, Andreas Hein / EyeEm, Axelle/Bauer-Griffin, Emad Aljumah, Deborah Kolb, monkeybusinessimages, Alexandr Sherstobitov, laflor, Michael Ochs Archives, Science Photo Library, BJI / Blue Jean Images, Dan MacMedan, ChrisHepburn, kzenon, Banar Fil Ardhi / EyeEm, PhotoAlto/Sigrid Olsson, Jade Albert Studio, Inc., New York Daily News Archive, Constantinos Kollias / EyeEm, Chris Walter, Photo by Claude-Olivier Marti, Kelly Cheng Travel Photography, Blend Images - Jose Luis Pelaez Inc, shapecharge, Compassionate Eye Foundation/Steven Errico, gbh007; HIGHRES PRESS STOCK/AbleStock.com; I. PREYSLER; ISTOCKPHOTO/ Getty Images Sales Spain; Devasahayam Chandra Dhas, Andreas Herpens, calvindexter, popovaphoto, Phazemedia, denphumi, SolStock, Pali Rao, JoeLena; J. M.ª BARRES; SHUTTERSTOCK/Glenn Copus/Evening Standard, Olivia Rutherford, MARIUS ALEXANDER, Iakov Filimonov, Sergey Novikov, Blend Images, terekhov igor; Farmer's Daughter; Jono Williams; Andrew Hyde; Aimee Giese; Museum of London; Samsung; SERIDEC PHOTOIMAGENES CD; Telegraph Media Group Limited; ARCHIVO SANTILLANA

**Cover Photo:** GETTY IMAGES SALES SPAIN/mixetto

**We would like to thank the following reviewers for their valuable feedback which has made Personal Best possible. We extend our thanks to the many teachers and students not mentioned here.**
Brad Bawtinheimer, Manuel Hidalgo, Paulo Dantas, Diana Bermúdez, Laura Gutiérrez, Hardy Griffin, Angi Conti, Christopher Morabito, Hande Kokce, Jorge Lobato, Leonardo Mercato, Mercilinda Ortiz, Wendy López

The Publisher has made every effort to trace the owner of copyright material; however, the Publisher will correct any involuntary omission at the earliest opportunity.